Cover Design by Walton Mendelson www.12on14.com
Photo by Jan Norden
Front Cover: Helene V Gross
Illustrations by Helene V. Gross

Library of Congress Cataloging-in-Publication Data available upon request.

To order more copies or to connect with the author/artist visit www.helenevgross.com.

Printed by CreateSpace, An amazon.com Company

Available from amazon.com, CreateSpace.com and other retail outlets

Available on Kindle and other devices.

I Am:

The Soul's Journey to Source..Within.

Helene V. Gross

Table of Contents:

Insight into the making of this book

What you are about to experience is the Journey I went through to complete this book. My Journey started many lifetimes ago but I was not aware of it. I knew I had a story to tell because every time I would mention bits and pieces of my life to someone they would stare in amazement and want to know more. This puzzled me because I didn't think it was all that amazing. I thought everybody had similar experiences. Some people said I had too much imagination and they called it daydreaming but I saw much of it became real, so for me it *was* real. When I placed my hands on people they would say in amazement that it felt hot or cold and some felt the subtle energy but almost all felt something. I thought it was completely normal, except for the responses I kept getting and I started to realize that I was different. Sometimes that was to my advantage and other times not.

I didn't know what to expect when I started school but the other kids and teachers didn't seem to have the same references as I did. My inquisitive mind was always wondering why this and why that. Teachers and parents weren't always appreciative of that, but it didn't stop me. I was curious and didn't stop at no. I continued until I got answers and some of the answers I got while sitting at the principal's office.

Looking back I feel I could not have done it differently (living my life). At times it was so rough that I almost gave up but you heard I said I 'almost gave up' but I kept going sometimes fast and sometimes slow but always in some form.

For some time my free spirit had to go 'in hiding' but when it emerged it shone brighter than ever and radiated the love that always was there.

Our light shines the brightest at birth because we have just come from Source and we are connected. It's like we have a hotline to the Divine Source and when we have lived down here on Earth for a while and have been taught how to behave or more correctly how to 'fit in' we loose a bit of the shine. We continue through life being filled with more and more 'stuff' until one day we 'wake up' and wonder what life is all about. Where is that person I once knew? You know the one that smiled and was happy and loving all the time?   Where am I? We are disillusioned and sad and wonder why? We look at old photos and wonder where the Spirit has gone? So for the rest of our lives we look for that connection again. We look for it in other people, beliefs or places.

The beauty of life, you find 'things' where you least expect it. I am not sure who wrote this...it could just be me ☺

And this is where we start our journey... I am 'connecting' to the above to take you guys on my journey...and we will be going places both known and unknown but don't you worry it will be the ride of your life (it has been a ride of my life)...so hop on this 'ship' with me. My story is a dialogue between my 'Universe/Multiverse/God/ Supreme Being/ Universal Intelligence/The Divine Source' or what you choose to call it, and *my-self*. Through this journey you will see my path unfolding before you, this is my path and my connection but by reading this book you will see clues to how YOU are connected as well... I will for easy recognition call it my Universe, even though we know we have multiple Universes often referred to as Multiverses.

The way-show-er = one who knows the way and shows it by being it. Knowledge= Self experienced truths.

Dear reader/ co-creator, what you have in your hand is a gem; you will be using it to find the essence of your life and you will need to read it more than once because for many of you, this is new stuff. There is nothing 'new' under the stars, but the guidance and timing are important and as long as you are open to it, it will set you free. You will be empowered and many subjects will be mentioned. They are the truths that are vital for this planet and her peoples survival. This book guides us to love one another and to live in truth and freedom.

The revelations in this book at first could be mind-boggling but you will see how true this is. It is also a 'how to' book so you can learn how to grow larger and healthier crops pesticide free for you to provide for your family and keep them healthy for generations to come.

We are thankful you took your time to educate yourself and when you are finished reading this book we would appreciate it if you would spread the information in this book. Through this 'silent' masterpiece we together can stop the madness happening and 'be' LOVE. Love will conquer not fear. We have lived far too long in fear and see where it has gotten us, nowhere. Now let's go in LOVE and be successful and turn this 'ship' around so we all can be happy and be able to sustain our families and communities and take back control of our lives. As you start to understand it takes so little and it is so simple too. Just a few principles to live by and we empower the worlds' people instead of giving our power away to greedy warmongers and people who don't care about us anyway. By reading this book and passing the information on we empower a whole world and by doing this we avoid extinction. The time is NOW, go in LOVE and spread it.

"We believe your words will reach millions of people and your life story will touch millions of people hearts. " The Universe

Will media scrutinize me if I include the hurt and abuse and all of these life-changing events that have occurred? I worry that the media will twist my words around and not represent the essence of what I want to tell in the book and maybe go for sensation instead of the truths. Who wants to know about my problems anyway, don't they have enough in their own lives? Me

No, because what you are writing about is your Journey, your connection to us, your 'Universe' throughout your journey and how that 'helped' you in many life situations.
When you speak your truth many people will come to see you and read your books.

I have reflected on these words directly above that I wrote at the start of this book and I am noticing my growth because 'worry' is something I don't do anymore. Worry is something I did in my past and now I ask myself, Does it work for me or not. When I see or hear about things that are' fear based' I call them out as they are. Why do we worry? How do we stop worrying? It is a choice we make, it is much better and gets better results to 'send love' to resolve it. Wow amazing reflection and it works!

> Your life has been very different from most, and you have had to suffer, but it has all been worth it. We believe in you and we know you will make the right decisions because you are LOVE. That is all you are going to be and have ever been, and will ever be.

How do I put this beautiful story you are reminding me of together with some of the negative things that have happened in my life? Even though it feels risky it does make sense to put it all out there. I just feel I am opening up myself to more than I feel comfortable telling. I like to be private and have few good friends who know me, they know the good the bad and the ugly, this is taking it to another level and it feels like I am exposing too much.

> They will understand that this book is just telling it like it is for no other reason than to enlighten people to seek their own enlightenment and to love all and to know we exist.
> In all of this you do remember we were there all the time, loving you and guiding you.

Yes I remember and when I look back, much of what 'happened' in my life could not have if you hadn't been there with me.

There are incidences in your life where you have been at crossroads and done things that were not that great, and it took a long time for you to find out what was right and wrong. We helped you go after what you felt was right and how you felt in your heart.

Do you not think you would be able to inspire people by telling your story?

Maybe…

You do it all the time….

I guess I don't always see 'the gift' of having direct communication like I have. I don't really know a life without it, except for when I was in deep turmoil. I know many times my connection with you was not clear and I haven't been able to follow the guidance because of conflicting thoughts. In some way I have always known that I would write a book I just didn't know it would be now. I knew I would not write a book if it did not have a bigger purpose which is what has been driving me all this time.

To do things just for fame or just for money has never been your gig. You always saw the bigger picture and always strived to give either love or to help others. Remember when you were 28 and we told you that it was time to stop helping everybody around you and start focusing on yourself?

Yes I do but it was not familiar for me to stop, so I continued.

We know, but we were trying to get you to 'help' yourself so you could get to this point that you are at now. We could see you were taking on all peoples 'stuff' and that it was stopping your own development. You were and are headstrong and you don't let anyone, not even us tell you what to do ☺

I agree! I am finally baaaaack, I know what I want and what I don't want and I have been letting other peoples wishes come before mine far too long. At first it was my first husband and my kids and even though I still will let my kids wishes come first, I am finished living my life like someone else wishes me to.

It is freeing to just be me and just do what I want. I wish that for everyone, to find the freedom to do what they want, to follow their heart and not do what they think they should.

To follow your heart is to be 'in the flow' and when you are in the flow magic happens. That is where you create and produce miracles. It is where scientists have 'come upon' life changing formulas and understandings. To understand it better it is like seeing yourself in slow-motion while you are going super fast and most of the sound is gone, physically that is what I experience when I am in the NOW, or in the FLOW. When I get out of it I miss it. But let's get on with the story...

Copenhagen, Denmark

<u>Happening:</u> Birth of girl, placed in the incubator, she has low weight, is premature and jaundiced, to an unmarried female who wants to put her up for adoption.

The earliest memory I have is when I was an infant looking up from the incubator and people standing around me looking down at me. I remember them shaking their heads as if they were sad and then turning around and leaving. I saw my baby hands reaching up towards them for a hug but everyone had left and I was alone.

Please tell me what you guys saw and did because I don't remember all the details of it. Could I see you guys, could I feel you? Did you calm me?

How your life started. Before we go any further we want to say that there is no beginning or end regarding the life of a Soul, it always is and always has been, but is only in different stages of life, put in terms people understand we start the book this way.

When we saw what was happening around you we knew we needed to act, and the way we needed to act was to make sure that you would come to your Grandfather's place because that's where the love was. You would have to deal with your Mother not wanting you, and your Father disappearing from your life. We thought that if you started your life with the love that your Grandfather and Grandmother gave you and the beauty and freedom and nature, we knew you would be a very strong being and we can see that now, with all the trials and difficulties you have had in your life, you get back up and go on.

You always go back to Skaerbaek Molle you always go back to your Grandfather's place and to your Grandfather's love. That is worth much more than anything.
Have you heard what happens to monkeys that are separated from their Mothers? They die if they don't get love even though they get food and everything. Love is very powerful and your Grandfathers love is what you hung on to all these years.

So in the beginning of the book, let us go in and say:

When you as a Soul came in from the constellation Orion, or more directly from the Star of Betelgeuse, you took a ride down into this human body. This human body (with you inside) your Mother, was doing everything she could to get rid of you, she ate very little, she drank alcohol and did vigorous exercises. She couldn't reveal that she was pregnant because she was in nursing school so by not eating or eating very little even at 7 months pregnancy it wasn't showing you were there.

You/your Soul were not sure you were ready for the mission you had given yourself before entering. You were in a state of chock because your Mother didn't want you, your Father didn't believe you were his and your existence was unsure. You decided you were going to live and when the birth happened, you were surrounded by us.

Where we come in, that you can remember in this lifetime, is when you are in the incubator when your hands are up in the air and the people that shook their heads had gone and you were alone. That's when we came in and showed ourselves to you. We had been around you the whole time, but when the people had gone and you brought up your hands, you were not bringing them up into thin air you did it because you wanted that love from us, that love came to you. That love took care of you, that love healed your heart, that love was familiar to you. We were all around you all the time and that is why you reached up for us because you saw us and felt us and we filled you up with love and light and beautiful energy.

So when your Grandfather said that he could see it in your eyes, it was because he could see *The Universe in your eyes*. He could see there was a power in you that he had not seen before. He had seen other newborns but nobody that shone like you

Grandparents intervene and 3 weeks later baby girl is in Grandparents place.

When your Grandfather saw you he immediately knew that there was something special with you and he put his foot down and so did your Grandmother and made sure you came home with them. The years you were with them were formative years. The love you received is what you are spreading to the world now.

Forward some years.

Helene is living the life with her wonderful Grandparents at their estate, running around in nature and becoming one with the birds, the dogs, the animals, the trees and streams and rivers that run through the estate. By feeling one with all and having the unconditional love from Grandfather and Grandmother, Helene develops into who she really is, <u>one with all</u>, radiating love to all. Being in this state was natural and it opened up all the wonders and miracles of life.

I remember being in this state of pure love. For me it was just the way I was and I never reflected on it.

Every morning I would ask my Grandfather if it was sunny outside, and if there were too many clouds or it was gray I would stay under the covers. I would stay in bed until breakfast was served. Otherwise I would jump right out of bed and spend my days running around outside exploring nature and feeling the sun on my skin, tasting the great ice cold spring water and letting it run through my fingers and drinking from my hands. For me it was the best tasting water in the world and if I could, I always drank it from my hands fresh out of the spring. I remember feeling one with Mother Earth, Father Sky and all the animals. Whenever I would lie in the grass listening to the (running) spring water I felt the energy and the magic of Mother Earth and I would look up to the sky and the clouds and sun. I felt she took care of me. I could lay there for hours just imagining all kinds of beauty. Whenever I would go for a walk in the forests I would know which animals would show them-selves, before they did. I had a kind of direct telepathic communication with them. I thought everybody did, and it was a natural state of being I was in.

Before going to bed at night I would 'transport' my-*self* into another state of mind, later on in life I realized it was called meditation, but I went everywhere in my 'state' and I had so much joy in that reality and for me it was real.

 I guess when we are <u>one with all</u> we are in total joy and bliss and my 'Universe' was my best friend. I did have some friends on the estate, their parents worked for my Grandfather and I played with them but most of the time I was roaming around in nature and playing with my cousins. I preferred being in nature because of the peace it gave me.

You see, ever since you were a little girl, you were looking up to the skies and feeling one with us.

Was I up on a higher frequency than I am now?

Yes. You were up there a lot and your heart was open and loving and it was a natural state for you to be in You are starting to get back up there now and you are experiencing the pure bliss again. We are happy you are getting to experience this again.

You loved everybody and everything.. Your Grandfather's wish was seeing you in this beautiful environment forever. He could not understand why he could not keep you in this pristine environment and let you be this free bird. He didn't really understand how much he had already done for you by just giving you that short amount of time. It was beautiful and exactly what you needed. You needed this place and this is the place you would always come back to when you were having a really hard time. This was your place; this was the beautiful magical place that you returned to when you were going through your toughest times.

Your Grandfather did you a huge favor, but he had to let you go because you had to go through all what you went through to grow. That was what you had 'chosen' as a Soul to experience in this lifetime. You needed to go through this to be able to understand all the difficulties people go through. You have a compassionate heart and understand the depths and difficulties people go through. That's part of your mission, you had to go through ups and downs and it's the downs that taught you the most, which is what you will help your fellow people to remember.

You see all that inhabit this Earth have chosen to be here and have chosen to 'forget' and then slowly remember why they are here. It is a process and by your book people will 'get it' faster.

When you totally trusted in us, (the move to Mexico) when everybody was telling you that it would be difficult but you said; " I am going anyway", that was beautiful.

But I already knew or felt I needed to be on this side of the 'pond'.

Yes, that's true, your Soul had already left and you already knew it. But on the other hand it was still beautiful that you totally trusted in us.

I had this very strong feeling that I was guided by a very strong force and it was so overwhelming that my doubt 'left' me. I know that I had periods where I had 'forgotten' or I was confused and couldn't listen to your guidance like when I was going through hardships.

So all you are doing now is taking all this 'crap' (my hardships)off of me which I have accumulated being down in this physical body. When I have gotten rid of this, can I shine again?

Yes, that's a good way of putting it. That is what we are doing. We are getting you back to your blueprint. By re-member-ing who you are you gain the ability to soar again.

You soared up there all the time, as a child.

Wow. Yes and I remember it.

You liked being up there, you could put yourself up there in no time. You just walked down the path to the river in Skaerbaek Molle and you were up there. That's why nothing ever happened to you. You were *one* with everything.

Being *one* with everything, is that a natural way of being? I am answering my own question because I never 'learned' to be *one* with everything, I just was.

That's why you were never scared and at this moment you are feeling that the fear is leaving you, you are not feeling that fear anymore. You are becoming the one you were.

I guess I am coming back to my 'blueprint' and that is to be *one*!

When I look around and see what people are going through I see they are separate from them-*selves* but don't see it. They are seeking to come back to them-*selves*. Without knowing it they are seeking it outside of them-*selves* and they will never find anything outside of them-*selves* except for fear and lack of love, lack of unity, lack of *one-ness*. Wow, what a revelation to know this or to remember this again. I feel my energy soaring just by these words.

"There is no reality except the one contained within us. That is why so many people live an unreal life. They take images outside them for reality and never allow the world within them to assert itself." Hermann Hesse.

To you dear readers/ co-creators, this is almost the end of my writing journey even though this is at the beginning of the book. I am having these great realizations☺ I have been through a great year and a half with all of these teachings that I needed to re-member to be able to write this book. By now you realize that I am talking to or conversing with my 'Universe' or God or Highest Being or Divine Source. I call them my 'Universe' even though I now know that I am really talking to ….when you finish this book you will know.
Back to the story.

We kept an eye on you and we kept filling you with love. When you pulled your fingers up towards us it was because you felt the love we were sending down to you. Those same hands are the ones that you are healing with today.

Those same hands are the ones that you took that dead bird with. Remember the dead bird?

I couldn't understand why it couldn't fly.

When you touched it you thought it would fly, and you gave it worms but it didn't move because it was dead. You believed all you needed to do was touch it and it would fly away. Like you healed the tree and it grew. You couldn't understand that it didn't work right away. You had to have that explained by your Grandfather, remember?

Yes.

We would come to you at nights up in your room when you were a little bit older, up in your room you would go into these other dimensions with us. You would look at the stars and you would know that we were there.

Was there a time when I almost drowned?

Yes, we had your dog help you out.

For real? Yes, because I thought it was in my imagination.

No, you did not make it up you actually fell in the water and you pulled yourself out with the dogs hair, the dog was with you.

I do remember there was something, just not the details.

What about the time you went looking for the hunter's dog. Do you remember the hunter that came to your Grandfathers estate asking if any one of you had seen his dog? You felt sorry for him and wanted to help so you and your cousins set out to find it.

Yes, I remember but they don't.

Well, Hanne fell in that square hole with water. Remember she was trying to jump over it and fell in.

Yes and it was cold. At that time we had been searching for hours but it was still light. After she fell in she wanted to go home but we were so far away and we were convinced that we would find the dog and that kept us going. I believe I was 5, Hanne was 7 and Gitte was 9. Wow we were doing these things at such an early age.

You guys kept going. You were never scared. Hanne and Gitte were scared but you were never scared even when it became dark. You just wanted to find that dog. When it was time to go home you knew how to get home, it was pitch dark but you knew your way home. You had been walking the whole day over streams, into the forests, over fields and everything and when it had gotten dark and it was time to go home you just turned around and said this is the way.

I remember I wanted to go get some help from some of the farms on the way but Hanne and Gitte were afraid that the people were bad people so we stayed away from the farms.

When Gitte said "no, this is the way" and Hanne said "no, this is the way", you said, "no this is the way' and in the end they followed you, even though you were the youngest. You knew the way because we were there with you. You just knew.

Wow.

The whole village and neighbors were looking for you and the dogs had already returned home.

I remember they left us because they wanted to get home and eat. I remember seeing them go.

They thought, ok you guys continue but we are going home.

Being afraid was nothing you really resonated with because you were not afraid and we were with you all the time so when you walked the forests we were there.

Hmmm.

And you knew there was a force beyond what people were talking about because you could see it. You looked at people as if they were square. Do you remember?

You could see things most people just didn't have a clue about, and when you looked at people you could see if they were good or bad. Your Grandfather knew that you knew.

People would come to him and you would go right up to them and say 'You are dumb' if you felt this person was not a good person. Your Grandfather paid attention, he would pay attention if this person was working for him and would keep an eye on him because he knew that what you said was right. You were his 'meter' of good or bad. You could do that with anybody. You looked at people and saw right through them. Don't you remember?

I am starting to remember now when you say it. I am remembering the feeling and seeing part. Wow I didn't have the blinders on then, did I?

Ok, but if I was able to see through people and I was completely open. Was I up on a higher frequency?

Yes. You were up on the higher frequencies and you were up there a lot.

You started closing down when you moved to Copenhagen with your Mother, because that's when doubt started coming in, that's when you started doubting yourself but until that time you didn't doubt yourself at all.

You were so open and saw everything so clearly that it was haunting for people who tried to hide things from you or from your Grandfather. You knew when people were playing nice and they weren't genuinely nice. Do you remember when you went around the factory and went to each one of the seamstresses that worked for your Grandfather?

Do you remember you went every single day and asked each one of them for candy or money? You knew when the bakery truck came with all the cookies and cakes, you wanted to buy some of them and your favorite was the French waffles with crème. Do you remember that?

Yes.

Do you also remember going up to Anderson who was your Grandfather's accountant and asking him for money?

Yes.

Your Grandfather would ask you, "Haven't you gotten any money from anyone else?" and you would say, "No". You would ask him too. He would say, "Hasn't Anderson given you anything either?" And you would say "no", so your Grandfather would give you some money too.

When the baker came, oh my, you would buy all the cakes you wanted. But of course your Grandfather knew that all the ladies had given you money and he also knew Anderson had, but they played along with you and you thought you were really smart and you were, but everybody knew your scheme.

They knew what you were doing but they thought it was fun, most of the seamstresses did. As you know not all the seamstresses thought it was fun, some of them thought you were spoiled, but that was just the way it was.

You played too, every night in the end when the TV was turned off you pretended that you were asleep. You had been watching TV the whole time but when they turned off the TV you closed your eyes and pretended to be asleep. Then you had your Grandfather carry you upstairs. Remember?

Yes I remember.

Well you didn't want to be up in that room by yourself and especially when it was cold in the winters.

I thought it was more fun being where everybody else was together in the living room and eating all the cookies I wanted. Nothing beat having my Grandfather carry me to bed. I felt that he needed to do that because it was that great feeling of his protection and his love that I loved. I remember falling asleep instantly after I was put to bed like that. Wow, what wonderful memories.

Do you remember the time when your Grandfather sent the cattle away for slaughter? You were so sad because you could feel their fear.

Well I remember how I cried and was mad at my Grandfather for doing it. It is a feeling I still get today when I pass the cattle trucks that I believe are going to slaughter. I feel the cattle and pray for them and I always cry.

Do you remember Krassus? The big English sheepdog, the dog that saved you from drowning, who was guarding you from the time you were an infant? He would sleep under the baby carriage and not let anyone near you except your Grandfather and Grandmother. Do you remember when he had to be shot because he had gotten sick? That was bad for you too.

Yes that was pretty traumatic and I remember how sad I was for the longest time. That dog followed me everywhere and I could always count on him for protection and companionship.

I remember the time I was chasing Krassus from the back of my Grandfathers factory. He was chasing a big ball and I was chasing him and we both ran full speed across the street. I remember out of my left eye I saw a black car coming straight at me but luckily it stopped in time. I remember my Grandfather coming out from the storage area furious and he smacked me in the behind. He had never laid a hand on me but I heard him saying later on that he had been standing looking out that window and witnessing this and thought I would die so his reaction was to slap me because he was so scared. Do you guys have anything to add?

We were there as well making sure you were unharmed. You know that at that angle and speed the driver could not have had the time to react under normal circumstances. So yes you have had some very close calls but we have been there the whole time making sure you were ok.

Are you telling me that under normal circumstances I would have died or at least been very hurt?

Yes. That driver did not see you because you were running right in front of him with such speed because you were chasing the dog who was chasing a ball and you ran out from the side of a building. There was no way the driver could have seen you until the very last minute. The driver swung away to avoid you, but he would later tell the story that something else had taken over his vehicle, because he had not reacted until the car had stopped. He would talk to your grandfather and many times reflect on what really happened there because he had not seen you.

Your Grandfather was so ashamed that he had laid a hand on you. He couldn't forgive himself for doing that. You were mad at him for a while because you didn't understand why he had hit you. He felt your confusion and he promised himself that he would never ever do that again.

Do you remember when he drove from the police?

Yes I do, but I never knew why.

He didn't want you to see him in a situation where he was not in control. He knew he had been speeding and that he would get a ticket or maybe his car would be impounded.

I remember this and from seeing him as invincible I changed how I saw him and thought he was a crook and I was mad at him for a long time. But he loved me so much that I couldn't be mad at him forever.

We were there as well making sure he got away, which he did.

Wow, so you guys have been protecting me all this time?

Yes, what did you expect!

I am not imagining this?

No, this IS your life and you have been protected for a reason that is unfolding right before your eyes.

Oh my God. I think I am beginning to understand it now.

Your life was beautiful but there were a lot of things that happened at the same time. When your Grandmother disappeared, she was in the hospital and she died and you couldn't understand where she was. Your family didn't want you to be upset. You didn't like that you didn't know where she was.

Then Helga moved in and you didn't like it and you said," No you can't move in here." "You can't be here." "You can't take Grandmother's purse." "That's Grandmother's purse." For a while you were not happy with Helga and your Grandfather had to come in and tell you that your Grandmother was in heaven and you couldn't understand that for a while. Then you opened up your heart for Helga too. She was a good woman.

The special attention you had enjoyed and the special care was changing because she was open and loving to everybody. She was a very beautiful loving woman. She treated everybody equal and she did not want you to have special treatment even though she knew you were special to your Grandfather. She knew how much your Grandfather loved you and she loved you too.

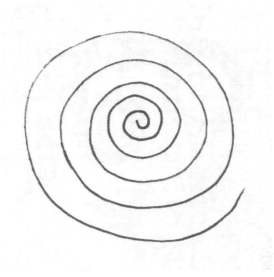

Year 6.

Before your Grandmother died she made your Mother promise that when she had settled down and started a family she would have you come live with her like a normal family.
The reason you were in Skaerbaek Molle all of those years was because your Grandfather's influence was vital. He showed you what unconditional love was. For the rest of your life you were more or less looking for that.

All of this was in the works without me knowing.
I only remember one incident when I was visiting my Mother in Copenhagen, my Grandmother was there with my Grandfather at the 'green house with the big garden'. I remember the grown ups arguing which up until that point I had never experienced.

Was that the time my Mother told my Grandfather that I was to go live with her in Copenhagen and go to school and then move to the US with her?

> Yes and that was when your Grandfather became furious. He left the house with you and your Grandmother and told your Mother that you belonged in Skaerbaek Molle. He realized after some time and legal counsel that he had no legal right to you and he also knew your Grandmother was sick at the time. Your Grandmother went to the hospital shortly after that.

My world changed and I moved to Copenhagen to live with my Mother and her sister.

> When you had your own room at your Grandfathers place you were able to connect with us every night. You were not able to do that when you lived in Copenhagen because Henrik was there. You couldn't let yourself go like you did then. Your Mothers sister, your Aunt loved you and helped you a lot. You knew you got love from her. She had always wanted a girl and she spoiled you by making you the most beautiful dresses. Violet was a favorite color of hers.

I remember a beautiful violet dress with a white rim and angel sleeves and a little 'Parisian' hat she made for me.

> Uncle Ole didn't understand you. He thought you were pretty spoiled. But you were very strong in yourself. Do you remember the time he called the home phone and you answered? And he asked you to present yourself to him and you said, "Ole, you know who I am." He wanted you to present yourself in a professional way and you were like, you know who I am and you kept saying that. You know who I am!

When he came home he was very mad that you couldn't present yourself and you were just confused, you said, "Onkel Ole, you know who I am! I don't need to present myself to you." He wanted you to present yourself and answer the phone in a certain way and you were very determined to answer the way you answered. That was part of who you were. Nobody could tell you how to do things because you did them your way.

When I moved to my Mother and Aunt in Copenhagen my Mother felt that I needed a firm upbringing. She seemed to think I had been very spoiled. She introduced me to 'rules', instead of what I was used to, unconditional love.

Everything I did and said was met with criticism.. There was nothing about me that she approved of. Being constantly corrected on what I said and did made me miss the wonderful flow I had with life at my Grandfathers. I felt like I was a round peg not fitting into a square hole. I felt confused and very unhappy and most of all perplexed that the wonderful life I had with my Grandfather could be so miserable with my Mother. I was very fortunate to have the love from my Aunt and she would defend me and get angry at my Mother for being too hard on me. I remember the feeling when my Mother looked at me in a disappointing way. I felt I was a misfit and it didn't matter if I had done something wrong or not, I felt guilty because of the way she looked at me without saying a word. I knew she disapproved of me. I struggled to find out how to please her unsuccessfully.

The reason is unfolding as well. Nothing is coincidence. You know that.

I understand that now but not then. At that young age to feel so unwanted and criticized at all times was devastating. I still had a very strong will and deep inner power and connection with all but the doubt was slowly creeping in.

27

My deep belief in myself instilled in me by my Grandfather made me question a lot of her decisions. I knew that when I moved away from my Aunt and my Grandfathers protection my life would be difficult. The few times I was alone with her is when I really saw who she was. It puzzled me that she despised me that much, when all I got from my Grandfather was unconditional love. I tried to be sure that I was never alone with her as much as I could.

I was old enough to go to school and my Mother enrolled me. At first I did my best to conform but then my 'self' would automatically go into 'me' mode and I would automatically question everything which always got me in trouble.. I don't really remember the other kids but I did remember the teachers. I asked a lot of questions and they asked me to be quiet and listen. I remember the feeling of being told what to do and I didn't like it. I couldn't wait for school to be over so I could go outside and be free with my thoughts and feelings and not have to pretend. I was curious and wanted to explore and experience all there was but here questioning was not appreciated.

Today I can see that I never liked 'rules' if I didn't understand them. I didn't care if they were rules made by grownups because I saw beyond that.

Richard Branson believes that rules are made to be broken. I agree.

Year 7: Going to America(Military Life).

America sounded so exciting and I looked forward to that adventure and at the same time I knew there were a lot of unknowns as well. What was my life going to be like without my Grandfather and Aunt?

My Grandfather came to visit me in Copenhagen about a month before we were to leave for the US and I said to him, "Grandfather, maybe Mother dies before we leave and then I don't have to go." I could feel he was very sad but he didn't want me to know this. I was very sad also but I pretended I was excited to go and part of me was but the other part was falling apart because I knew I would miss him. I felt I had to do my best to adapt to this new life and people around me seemed to think it was a big deal so I looked forward to it.

Do you remember the time you boarded the plane going to the US and you all were late, and the plane had to wait?

Yes and I remember just before exiting from my Aunt's place Henrik and I had an argument and somehow my Native American necklace broke with thousands of beads flying all over the place and I refused to go anywhere until I had all the beads with me. That was why we were late. I wouldn't go unless I had them with me. That was how strong I was.

And when the flight was close to New York City you were greeted with a thunder and lightning storm and for two hours the plane tried to land at JFK and all it could do was circle over New York until the storm ceased. The oxygen masks were released and the rest of the passengers in the airplane were in a panic state while you were just fine and not the least bit scared. You knew we were there with you and you knew you were going to be fine. You just knew you had that protection and there was no question that you would be fine.

Wow, yes I do remember not being afraid and couldn't understand why others were. I just knew we were going to be alright without a doubt. I looked at them and wondered what they were afraid of. I didn't resonate with fear as a young child, it was foreign to me.

I also remember my first day in New York. After our arrival from Denmark we were going to meet Tony in another part of JFK and it took a while until we found him. Then we went to pick up our new Swedish bright turquoise colored Volvo my Mother had purchased and it wouldn't start. We eventually got it started some hours later and drove through New York. It was very exciting to see this new place, which in some way felt familiar to me. I knew I had never been there in this lifetime, but somehow it was familiar. When we drove through New York I could see the playgrounds with children playing. I wanted to go play with them but I was told this was not the best side of town to stop in. This was new for me, I was not familiar with that kind of thinking and again fear was not part of my life. We were looking for Tonys' Aunts place and then when we found it, I saw it was a high-rise and I got all excited. I had never been in a high-rise before. I imagined that when looking out the window it would be like looking out the window from an airplane while it was in the air and the cars would be the size of matchbox cars. I didn't hesitate to run to the balcony as soon as we arrived inside her apartment. I looked over the balcony and saw some people inside our car and told Tony about it. He and his nephew ran to the elevator as fast as they could, they got downstairs and when they reached the car the people had already broken in and taken jewelry and money that had been left behind. I heard his nephew say we were lucky they hadn't taken all the wheels. I don't remember the details, only that I thought this was an exciting place. Wow what a start of a new life.

We stayed at Tonys' Aunt place for some days and then it was time to travel to the military base where Tony was stationed. It took several days drive to get to Fort Benjamin Harrison, Indiana. After we got ourselves situated, the first chance I had I wanted to go out and play and ran to the playgrounds. My first encounter with American children was a bit 'frightening' for the lack of a better word. I was at the playground behind my house and one kid asked me what my name was, I didn't understand him and said, "No." Then I ran all the way home and asked my Mother what, "What is your name?" meant and when I heard what it meant I felt so ashamed that I had answered 'no'.

I came to a country that didn't understand my language and I didn't understand theirs, but it only took me about three weeks until I was fluent in English.

We were there with you in Indiana at the Military base when you had to learn the language very fast.

Did I mention that my life was changing dramatically? My 'Step Dad' wanted me to call him Dad, which I thought was strange since I had never called anyone Dad before and I hardly knew him. It didn't feel right but if he wanted it I could agree to that as well. I had a half sister and brother much younger than myself who needed much attention. My life was so different in so many ways. I really missed my Grandfather and I would think of him daily. I wanted to be with him.

Later on in life I learned that my Grandfather stopped celebrating Christmas for years because I had been taken away. He didn't see any joy in life since I was not there with him. Wow, that was love. On the other side of the Atlantic Ocean I was crying many years because I longed to be back with him. I would lie in my bed and transport myself back to his place ☺

We knew you would be a very strong being and we can see that now, with all the trials and difficulties you have had in your life you always go back to Skaerbaek Molle, you always go back to your Grandfathers place and to your Grandfather's love. That is worth much more than anything.

It seemed so distant but I kept believing that one day I would be reunited with my Grandfather and everything would be alright again. Life on Military bases was fun for kids. There were so many other kids to play with and it was quite a safe environment. I knew not all people would experience what I experienced so I was grateful to get to know people of all color and races and cultures. The Military provided this by us living so close to people from all over the world.

31

When we moved in I understood very soon that people and families were moving in and out all the time. So being the new kid in class was just part of the whole experience. Families were constantly moving in or out and stationed in this country or others. It was never boring and people were not set in their ways because you had to adapt to new places and people all the time. It was a feeling of constant change and I liked it. I remember most of the families were nice.

Sundays we had parades and BBQ and baseball games.

New people would be moving in and new acquaintances were made. I learned very fast through experience that your friend today could move tomorrow without warning. I met this Korean girl at school and she sat next to me and we became friends right away and then one morning she was gone and I never heard from her again. I learned to not attach myself to anyone too deeply because they could disappear without warning. I still sometimes wonder where she is.

Year 11: Civilian Life.

We moved out from the military life and on to civilian life. We moved from Ft. Benjamin Harrison Indiana to Wisconsin across from 8 tennis courts and I become obsessed with tennis. I 'inherited' an old broken wooden racket with a clamp on it and spent as much time as possible on the courts. I loved tennis and couldn't get enough of it.

> Sometimes we came in when you were playing tennis and we were watching you from the sidelines.

I really loved the game. When I hit winners I almost knew you guys were there.

You really hit that ball hard but because the racket was broken and had a clamp on it you would either hit winners or it would go out of the court.

I know and it was a bit embarrassing and some girls looked at me and wondered if it was really ok to play with a broken racket. I always pretended that it didn't bother me.

Yes, you loved the game so much that you looked at it from the positive side and felt blessed that you were even playing the game.

Civilian life was a bit different from Military life. For starters, my Mother was terrified of us kids being kidnapped. When we would go shopping she would be very stern about us always being close to her so she could see us. The parking lots were her big fear. I remember looking at her and wondering why this fear would be so strong with her, but trying to understand her was difficult, so I just tried to conform to her rules. I always had a question for every situation but she didn't always appreciate that. Just like the teachers didn't always appreciate my questions so I was often sent up to the principals' office. Unfortunately being sent to the principals' office also required for me to explain to my Mother and Step Dad what I had done wrong and most of the time I couldn't explain and didn't understand that there was anything wrong with asking questions.

It was not that I was being a 'bad' girl, I just wanted to know why things had to be done in a certain way.
Today, I understand on a deeper level why I kept on asking. I was not satisfied with the answers and knew when I was being mislead or when someone was trying to hush me up. Back then I was labeled an unruly kid by my fourth grade teacher.

We were also watching you when you went to Edgewood Elementary School, you had trouble with that teacher. She was the first teacher you really had trouble with, otherwise you had pretty nice teachers.

When you moved to the house is when things deteriorated. You loved   nature, the big trees, and so on and that's when you started healing trees.

Do you remember the branch that was broken? You went and put tape around it and you put your hand around it and said, "You are going to be fine." The tree grew and the branch grew strong. You saw that you could do things like that.

We also helped you with the household chores. You felt it was unfair you had to wash the floors and do all the laundry while your Mother was sitting and reading the paper or watching the daytime soap operas. You felt it was not fair but you did the dishes and everything without protesting.

Things turned from bad to worse. My Mother gets a call from Denmark. Her brother had been in an accident and survived but his wife was killed and their 4 children suddenly had no Mother. My Mother leaves for Denmark to help out her brother.

At the time I was 12-13 years old and I get the responsibility of taking care of my little brother and sister and the house while Tony was at work. The strained relationship I had with Tony takes a turn for the worse.
He abuses me physically and sexually and shuts me up with threats that he will kill me if I ever told anyone. Needless to say my world totally collapsed. My grades and my behavior at school turned south. I couldn't concentrate and I was in constant fear. I couldn't think straight and I had no one to turn to. My world shattered .

The evenings were the worst because he was home and my siblings were asleep. When I tried to sleep I couldn't and lay awake and was paralyzed under the covers knowing that it was only a matter of time before he would silently come into my room and go to my bed. It didn't matter if I was pleading with him not to; he told me that the girls in Vietnam my age were doing it. I screamed and he just held his hand over my mouth. I sort of left my body while this was going on and I felt there was someone who was protecting me and 'taking me away'.

It was as if I was being taken to a faraway land with a lot of loving people and I remembered it from the feeling I had at my Grandfathers place.

We came in and helped you when you were being abused. We didn't really help you; we could just take you away into another dimension.

After the assault I would have this feeling of 'ok its over for now but when will it happen again' and pleading for it to stop.

Oh how I missed you guys. I really wanted to have the connection again with you.

You did have the connection but you were in so much turmoil that you could not be calm and enjoy as you did before. You felt we had left you and you felt alone and you missed your Grandfather even more because you saw him as your protector. You prayed that you would be with him soon.

My teachers were complaining to Tony about my behavior because I wasn't listening and was talking too much. I couldn't concentrate on anything for longer periods of time because I was hiding this big secret and had no one to turn to. My mind was in a state of shock and I could not think one thought clearly. This fear was eating me alive, it was a constant uneasy deep dark feeling. From being fearless to this was so disturbing for me because I knew what was happening was wrong but I didn't see any way out and nobody I could rely on.

At least when I was in school I felt a little more at ease because I was away from home and could escape into the other reality. The teachers just understood that I wasn't paying attention.

None of the teachers even stopped to ask what was going on instead they just blamed me and gave me a hard time.

More than once the teachers would ask me questions to test me if I had listened and I would take a split second and come down and answer correctly. I remember I would be out 'in orbit' and hear the last part of the question and somehow get the answer right.

You know we helped you, right?

Well I figured that, because in many situations I knew I couldn't possibly have known these things that were asked and I would have the correct answers often.

When they assigned us to do homework I would forget and many times not even have known or heard what they had said for us to do.

It was a horrible time and when my Mother returned she heard of the trouble I had caused at school and the dropping grades from straight A's to D's so she suggested I get counseling. I went to get my brain hooked up to an electroencephalogram (EEG) machine to check my brainwaves and see what was wrong. The doctor had one talk with me afterwards and then wanted to talk to Tony right away, which never happened. Tony had served in Korea twice and once in Vietnam and one of his duties was to 'interrogate' prisoners. He had just retired from the Army and of course he made everyone believe I was the liar, but I found it interesting that the counselor wanted to speak to him right away.

Having my Mother at home made the sexual abuse cease but he kept going to my room at nights, I could feel his presence but pretended to sleep.
I felt uneasy being near him. He would hug me but I wanted to be as far away from him as possible.

On Sunday mornings the whole family would gather in the Master Bedroom except me. I would stand outside listening to the fun my siblings and Mother and Tony would have. I prayed the day would be a happy one. I was expected to make all the beds and mop the floors before breakfast and then do all the dishes afterwards. The time I enjoyed was when I would be outside on the lawnmower all weekend and just cut the grass and be away from everybody.

I kept disappearing into these dimensions and what I call the other realities to get rid of my tensions because even though the abuse had stopped I was still 'living them' over and over again. I was numb to the outside world and my only sanity was when I would 'disappear into this reality' it would give me some peace. While this was going on I would also pray every day, to come home to my Grandfather's place. That he was alive was my only hope and my only lifeline. I tried to write a dairy in code so that nobody would understand but me, and my Mother found it. Since it was written in code she didn't get alarmed about it.

You may go up in your Akashic Records if you have any questions.

I would like to know why I didn't tell my Grandfather that I needed him. I know that when I wrote letters to him my Mother would read them before sending them so I couldn't really tell him. Why didn't I contact the school or anybody who could have helped me? Why did I feel I could not go to anybody or trust anybody with what was happening to me?

We see this keeps you in a state of not trusting anyone and not trusting yourself in some way.

Yes, it does.

This is a previous lifetime pattern that you have had to conquer in this lifetime.

I didn't think past lifetimes were that important to this one.

Well, past lives can put light onto your types of behavior. Past lives can make you better understand who you are today. They show you what happened then and let you know that this is something that has happened before and this is how you reacted. Through that you can learn that it is a pattern you do not need to keep, and it gives you the ok to break the pattern once and for all.

Wow, so that means when we become aware of past life patterns that have gone over to this life we see what works and what doesn't. We

can then choose to abort the pattern and change our ways because then we see that it is part of what we have 'inherited' from before.

Yes, that is how it works.

Ok back to the story...

My disintegrating grades continued and my ability to concentrate worsened. This constant fear kept me 'paralyzed'. Even though the sexual abuse had ceased, I never knew what would happen around the corner. I could never let myself relax. I would do things and 'accidents' would happen that I was punished for. If it wasn't Tony who got mad at me it was my Mother who was on me instead.

Do you remember us coming to you and 'taking you' away?

I remember sometimes feeling a bit better but always on the lookout for him. I remember my keen sense of feeling and very sharp hearing. I could sense when peoples' energy or thoughts were directed towards me.

You could hear what people thought as well.

I could?

Yes, don't you remember?

Well some of it I remember, but I doubted my abilities because of all of this abuse.

Yes we know.

Then my Mother gets this brilliant idea (I say sarcastically) that she was going to work at a gift shop some evenings and again my world collapsed. I tried to find a way to run away. One evening I just slipped out the door after I had done the dishes and started walking into the back forest. It was dark but I just kept walking, I felt that anything that could happen in the wild could not be worse than what was happening at my home. I am not sure how long I was away but I heard my Mother call for me and she sounded worried.

In the end I was found and scolded and was told to go to bed. The following days after the incident, she was nice to me and let me off the hook, but soon it was back to screaming at me because of this and that and slapping me around. This was my daily treatment.

One night I had a dream that I was walking out of my room and down the stairs and my Mother came out and stopped me and told me to return to my room. The next day my Mother asked me where I was going. I was surprised she knew what I had been dreaming about and then I realized I had been sleepwalking and that seemed to worry her.

For some days she treated me well but soon it was back to normal, with her abuse and scolding me 24/7 for everything and nothing. Besides the physical abuse there was the psychological abuse as well. I couldn't turn anywhere for help and I was quite isolated.

You had your refuge outside in nature. Do you remember the tree you loved to climb? When you were in that tree we connected with you.

Yes, I do remember that. It was the only place I felt one with all again. I really loved climbing trees, I was a natural.

Yes you were, just like when you lived at your Grandfathers place. You were always climbing trees. When he went looking for you he would have to look up in the tallest trees and there you were.

One day at school somebody's lunch ticket had gone missing and the teacher asked all the students if anyone had seen it. The kids figured I had taken it because that day I had bought lunch and I usually had my lunch bag from home.
I had not told them that every day my mom gave me milk money and I saved it so I could have one bought lunch once in a while and while I was innocent my teacher called my Mother and Tony and I got in so much trouble. I got home and my Mother started interrogating me for about 6 hours. She kept hitting me every time she asked and I told her I hadn't stolen the lunch ticket. Then she asked how I was able to buy lunch and I didn't tell her that I would save the milk money because then I was afraid I wouldn't get that either. My only comfort in all this was that when all of this had passed I could continue to buy lunch once in a while. I was not about to give up my milk money.
In her defense I understand where she was coming from. How was I able to buy lunch when I did not get any money from home? She was furious and slapped me and screamed at me and I kept saying I am innocent.

In that 6 hours I realized that I had nobody on my side and I also realized my situation was becoming dangerously out of control. When I looked into her eyes I saw evil but I also saw she couldn't control me and that made her even angrier. She threatened me and said she would tell Tony and while she was hitting me I got 'taken away' from this by my 'universe' and for a while I was physically standing there but not feeling the hurt. She realized I had 'gone' and got even more furious. She went into a rage and started beating me and screaming her lungs out, I 'came back' and now I saw my life could be in danger. She was so out of it and really mad and I knew the worst had yet to come.

> Yes dear ONE we were there 'taking you out' and we were so taken by your stamina. You were not going to let go of the little joys you had by admitting to something you hadn't done and we were proud of you for keeping quiet about the milk money. We saw then that you were tough.

When Tony came home she told him, he took out his belt and I must have been taken 'out' again because I don't remember anymore. I just remember that I couldn't sit on my behind because it was bloody and I had to be excused from PE for weeks because of my bruises and sores. I don't remember how long before I could shower with the other girls again but I do remember my Mother and Tony forcing me to go to school and admitting that I had stolen the ticket in front of the class when I knew I was innocent.

That was so humiliating and that left a mark for life. Of course the physical and sexual abuse left marks as well but since I have been dealing with that trauma for years now and have been healing that wound, it wasn't until I started writing this book that I was again experiencing the ticket incident and really understanding what turmoil my life was in and how it affected my life.
It made me a more conscious parent (of course my kids may disagree, like we know kids do) and I would never have my children put in such a horrible situation. My children always came before me. I would defend them even though I knew it could be their fault. I would always be on their side in any case and I would never doubt them and their integrity not even if it was against the King or President.

Now when I go back to the scene, I am amazed at the resilience I had as a youngster and the strength and willpower I had to go through this. Somehow I knew there would be brighter days ahead so I kept going.

Can you tell me something about me always being picked on and not really defending myself and not saying anything about what was happening in the states to any official? Why didn't I do that? I was scared stiff yes but at the same time I knew it was wrong.

We came to help you in those situations and took you away from them in many ways. Since this was *your lesson* and since this was something you had *chosen* to experience you did not stand up for yourself until you felt you could. You still showed love and respect to the people who hurt you and you had a very hard time understanding why this was happening to you. But we want you to know that you have taken many years to get over it but you are over it. We've been there the whole time loving you and we are sorry to see the fact that your Grandfather had a suspicious feeling that something was not right with you. He is very unhappy that you didn't tell him and at the same time he understands you. You loved him so much that you didn't want him to feel hurt. You see, that's how powerful you are, you would not tell him what had happened. You would not reveal it to anybody until he was not around anymore that is how much you love your Grandfather. You knew it would have broken his heart and he knows too. He is also very proud of you that you have come through that too.

You see you are a warrior. You are that warrior you always have been. You have been through worse than this, this is just this life....

Hmm.

43

You have been a slave before….

Wow.

So the years went and we moved to Puerto Rico and were living in the tropics and my Grandfather wanted desperately to see me so he sent tickets for the whole family to visit Denmark for summer vacation and I felt, this is the best present of my life. When I arrived in Denmark and my Grandfather greeted me, I cried. I was so happy to be with him at last. We went to the estate and I saw some of my old friends and one day he took me out to drive and asked me if Tony had treated me like a father. I felt I couldn't say no, so I changed the subject, and asked him if I could stay with him. He talked to my Mother and arranged for me to stay.

We helped you in 1978 when you came back to Denmark and you didn't want to return with your Mother and your siblings to the US.

When the vacation was over my Mother and my siblings went back to the US and I was so happy to stay in Denmark.

Year 15: Back in Denmark.

Look at this, I am 15 years old and I want to be as far away from Tony and my Mother as possible and the only place I feel safe is with my Grandfather. I felt I could breathe and just 'be me' again. I did miss the US but I had a feeling I would return later.

Being back in my paradise and enjoying the rest of the summer free from my Mother's tyranny and being with my beloved Grandfather was priceless. My cousins were here and so were my friends and I was so happy. I had my freedom again and was in my sanctuary. I started singing again and living that magical life like before, but I appreciated it so much more because I had experienced the darkness.   Once in a while the past bad memories would creep up to the surface and I would do all I could to put them back down. My Grandfather would take me for a lot of rides when he conducted business and many times he would ask if Tony had treated me like a father. I hated that he asked because it would make me remember. I felt I was never far away from it, I felt I could never escape it, the memories and the hurt never really left me.   I was always hesitant in telling my Grandfather what really happened, so I didn't. I just said; "Yes."

Ok guys, why didn't I tell my grandfather? Why wasn't I able to confront him and my school with what had happened? What stopped me from doing that?

Your own fear that nobody would believe you stopped you.

So fear stopped me? Part of me didn't feel my Grandfather would be able to handle it either. He was not young anymore. I could see that.

Well you felt you were partially guilty. You played the game in some way.

And your Mother was not there for you, nor has she ever been there for you.

Do you remember when you told her about it?

45

Yes. It was after she had divorced Tony and came to my Grandfathers place to live. She didn't believe me and got angry at me and told me to shut up and stop lying. I remember that I was very vulnerable and needed to confide in her but she verbally attacked me and that made me shut up for a while.

So you created this to in some way stop this from happening again.

Has this happened before, have I been molested, in my past lives?

Yes, many times and that was why it was 'so familiar' to you.

Oh my God…That sounds unbelievable. You are saying that because of a familiar feeling from past lifetimes I didn't stand up for myself?

Yes, that is how important past lifetimes can be for the present life.

Your relationship with your Mom started many lifetimes ago and before you two (souls) decided to come down to this earth you two made an agreement. The agreement was that she was going to teach you all about love, but the way she was going to do that was for you to experience the *opposite of love*, for you to grow as a human being.

Wow, going back, so my feeling guilty of 'cooperating' (by not daring to scream too loud) even though I knew he was wrong to be doing what he did. Even though I had screamed nobody would have heard me anyway, except my siblings who were asleep. We lived so far away from other neighbors that they wouldn't have heard.

I didn't have the guts to tell anyone because Tony had made sure I was afraid of the consequences if I ever told anybody, so I kept quiet. He told me he would 'skin' me alive. I did not know what that meant but it sounded horrific. Wow, I remember not knowing who to turn to. I wondered who I could count on to help me and believe me. I knew that *if* I told anybody it was imperative that they believe me right away or else my life would be in even more danger. Tony had done a great job of making people believe that I was a liar, by pointing out when I told 'stories'.

Little did he or anyone else know that they were the 'happenings' I experienced when I went into the other dimensions. I didn't defend myself because I didn't feel I would be believed. I remember seeing through him and seeing how fake he was and how little he was, but at the same time I was afraid of him, of what he was capable of doing to me.

At that point I couldn't see how powerful I was because my 'self' had taken such a blow from both my Mother and Tony. I remember just being in survival mode. I kept juggling the 'stuff' that was constantly coming at me from all directions, the criticism, the ridicule and the abuse that was my everyday reality. My sense of security was gone and I prayed all the time that I would be with my Grandfather as soon as it was possible.

It was silent prayers that I would say each night to get me out of this hell.

After so many years in the state of survival mode I was elated to be back with him again. I don't know how to explain it better than to say I felt I was let out of prison. It was so fantastic that I remember pinching myself and crying out of happiness. Walking the grounds at my Grandfather's place with all the familiar people and loving surroundings I was the happiest I had been in a very long time.

Today I regard my Grandfather as a hero and a savior. My sanctuary was Skaerbaek Molle with my Grandfather. I see how people who have nobody must struggle and I thank my 'Universe' for being there all this time.

It is fun to see the 'coincidences' like when I started school in Denmark I ended up in the same class my Grandfather had enrolled me in when I was a first grader all those years ago because he wanted me to stay with him. The principal told me that they had been waiting for me to come back 'home'. I saw how free the kids were in school, and how liberated they were. You could say just about everything without being judged and it was freeing.

At school I was the kid from America and I remember almost sleeping through English class, but having to learn Danish from the bottom up. I stayed at my Grandfather's for the remaining years and enjoyed every bit of my freedom.

After a while I was beginning to feel restless and on my 17th year I wanted to be in the center of where all happened so I moved to Copenhagen, well I was in Copenhagen during the weekends and in the North of Copenhagen during the week. The 'past nightmares' were surfacing and I felt I needed to be in the big city. If my Grandfather could choose he would want me to go to Alderup Gymnastics School like he and my mother had gone, but I had other plans.

I 'ran around' like many people do with an empty heart. I was looking for answers outside of me. I was looking for love, for acceptance, for someone to fall in love with. I looked for the prince who would sweep me off my feet and take me away with him into the sunset and then live happily ever after.

I see I was searching for someone outside of me to make it all go away. I met a lot of 'frogs' with a lot of promises and who said they could help but it all had a price and that was not anything I wanted to partake in. My life was a bit dark and my Grandfather tried to help but he just wanted me to go back to his place and I just couldn't. I needed to move on.

We watched over you when you were in Copenhagen. You were quite daring walking back home in the middle of the night after dancing to the music. You loved to dance and you preferred to dance alone and get into the groove.

My outlet would be dancing and music and I needed that.
I would meet my Grandfather on the weekends for breakfast in Copenhagen and we would talk. He was worried about me being in the city but I wanted to stay because it was fun and I met a lot of people. I would stay at my cousins place which was right in the middle of the city.

I did have some really fun times and looking back I see there was no other way for me to have coped with it all.

Year 18: Trip to Jordan.

Denmark was allowing people from many arab countries come and live. I have always been fascinated with other cultures. I went to explore the Arabic countries. Today I still wonder how I made it out alive. Again I was not scared, but looking at it with my 'grown up' eyes; I am amazed how smooth all went.
On my travel our tour guide advised us not to eat too much kebab, but I found a 'hole in the wall' type place that served great kebab and it was so good. Prior to that I had never eaten kebab and with my healthy appetite I couldn't help myself. I got so sick I had to go to the hospital and have my stomach pumped. The hospital wanted to know if I had money to pay for the stay and asked if I was going to be staying in 1st, 2nd or 3rd class and I said 1st. I was admitted and they started talking about taking out my appendix. I was losing my conscience but before I did I said it was not my appendix and when I woke up the next morning I was glad I still had my body intact.
I remember waking up in a foreign country but ok with it and I wasn't going to call my family and tell them my predicament because I didn't

want them to worry. I felt I was watched over by my people my 'Universe', whom I later named them.

> We were also there when you were in Jordan and when you were in the hospital. We were there making sure that you actually got the treatment that you needed.

I thank you guys for that. I remember talking to the only doctor who spoke English, what a 'coincidence' that he was on duty.. I say laughing.

> Like you know there is no such thing as coincidence, it is called synchronicity right? Things happen because we/you create them.

Outside my hospital room there was a lot of commotion going on and suddenly a man popped in who had the most beautiful green eyes I had ever seen. He smiled and I felt like this was the worst timing in the world. I knew I looked like a ghost and I needed to get out of my bed and get washed up. The nurse came by later on and helped me. He popped by in the evening and said his sister had had her appendix taken out. I remember thinking that I was glad they hadn't taken out my appendix.
He came in with a little bouquet of flowers and asked if he could help me with anything. I had never seen anyone with such beautiful eyes and such a kind smile I was pretty speechless and at the same time flattered, and still nauseous and sick. He kept visiting me every day and when I was ready to leave the hospital, he asked if he could give me a lift back to the hotel. I was delighted and said yes. He took me on a sightseeing trip around Amman and played beautiful songs in the car and we sang together. He had a beautiful voice and everything about him was magical. The whole experience was surreal and I was just sucking in all the beauty and the beautiful energy.

While we were driving, his demeanor changed and I wondered why. He said the police did not allow people of the opposite sex that are not married or related to be in the same car. Being blond made me a target so we had to be extra careful.

I am thinking that the tinted windows of today would have solved that problem.. I was a bit surprised at this rule.

He dropped me off at the hotel and helped me with the luggage and the doorman gave me a dirty look. I felt it and I understood that what the doorman saw and assumed was not what was happening but it could easily be misinterpreted. 'My knight in shining armor' said that we had to be careful not to be seen together because we could be thrown in jail. I could not imagine living in a country with that much control. It did not frighten me which I see now it should have, but made me even want to see more of what this was all about. It perplexed me that people could 'surrender' to that kind of life. I could not get out of my head the fact that being a female meant that you were a second rate citizen and was treated like you did not have a mind of your own.

He called me later when I had settled down and asked if I would like to go sightseeing the next day. Of course I wanted to see as much as possible. The way he looked at me made me feel like I was the most beautiful person on this planet. I knew I was afraid of falling for him, which I see now, that I did. I knew in my mind of course the magic was going to end as I was leaving for Denmark and I needed to see reality and also see that this man was of another culture and belief and I needed to go home. Before leaving I gave him my gold heart necklace which was given to me by my Grandmother. This was my most precious piece of jewelry and still today I think of it and know I wouldn't have given him this if I didn't feel that love for him. It even perplexed me that a person could affect me so strongly in such a short time. I cried all the way home in the plane but knew it was the right decision in the long run.

He had my number and kept calling me for about a year and in the end I had my Grandparents taking the phone because it was too painful to talk to him.

I was enamored by him but my rational mind didn't let me get too involved. I have always wanted to see him again and really hope he has had a joy filled life. I almost ran into him in Amsterdam in 1991. Royal Jordanian Airlines were staying at the same hotel and he was not among the crew but I did speak to one stewardess who had heard him speaking about me. At that time I believe he had been married. We could have met if he had been working. Thinking about him I know that that kind of love is rare and I appreciate that I was able to experience it. Looking back I knew falling for him was out of the question because of the different culture regarding the way women were regarded.

He didn't look at it that way but that was how people saw it who lived there. At the time my heart had such a deep wound and hole in it that I felt vulnerable. Too many incidences pointed to disaster if I would have stayed, one of them being losing my ' freedom of speech' so I never totally gave it a chance. I knew if I had stayed I would have challenged all the rules and I would have been in very deep trouble. The way I thought at the time and the way my new found freedom in Denmark made me feel I just couldn't imagine living that kind of life where I would be a second class citizen and who knows maybe we would never even have gotten that far but I was not giving it a chance..

Year 19.

Back in Copenhagen at a party I decided to go home early, well early in the wee hours after midnight, and I was on my way past the Hotel D'Anglettere and was stopped by a man in a car who happened to see which predicament I was in (I had broken a heal but walked as if I was just fine) but he was persistent and wanted to drive me home. I told him I was staying right around the corner, and that I was meeting with my Grandfather in a few hours for breakfast. He had a hard time believing me but I was persistent. We met again weeks later in Sweden and we fell for each other.

I moved up to Sweden, and we lived together and traveled. Our first trip was a trip to Israel. We were invited to a friends wedding in Tel Aviv. What an experience. Before the wedding we did a bit of sightseeing and went to the Dead Sea and after that to Jerusalem. It was a time of unrest so we were not able to go to the Wailing Wall but we could see it from a distance. Our friends took us to see many other holy places and experience the real Israel. I remember the great feeling I felt being in this wonderful country, the energy was very strong and positive. It was an energy filled with hope and love. The wedding was fantastic, one of the most fun weddings I had ever attended.

After our trip he wanted to get serious and started talking about having kids. I believe we were together about a half year before I got pregnant.

He wanted kids and I felt we could wait but he was adamant and we tried and just like I already knew we were 'preggo' right away. Before my pregnancy he was with me every minute of the day but as soon as I got pregnant his behavior changed and he was 'working' odd hours and never seemed to be home at night.

We would go to sleep and I would wake up and the bed would be empty and when I looked around the house was empty. I had not had that experience before and since my relationship with my Mother was strained I didn't feel I could confide in her. I talked to my Aunt but not about the fact that he was absent at night. I was actually ashamed of his behavior and I didn't know what to do about it. I felt vulnerable.

I loved the feeling of pregnancy and couldn't wait till I met the baby growing inside of me. Most of all I wanted this to work and I loved him and he said he loved me and that I was the most beautiful woman in the world. I guess I kept going and believed him but something was nagging at me. I was young and I tried to tell myself that he needed his freedom I knew how much my freedom meant to me and I wanted all to be alright. I hoped love could dissolve the pain.

During the last part of my pregnancy I was desperate to find out what he was doing so one night I pretended to fall asleep and when he got out of bed I did too. He was surprised that I was all dressed and I said I wanted to go with him, wherever he was going. He drove me around the city and then drove home. I went back to bed and being pregnant I was very tired so I fell asleep. I believe he did too that night, but soon again he was off at odd hours again.

I remember one special morning, the sun was up and it was the morning I gave birth to my daughter. He came home at 6AM and I told him that we needed to go to the hospital right away. We went and when my daughter was born and was healthy, I told myself and promised the 'Universe' she was going to have a biological Mother and Father and be loved unconditionally.

While I was in the birthing room I felt the 'Universe' had opened up and I had direct contact with the above and it was a fantastic feeling. My connection with the above was very strong and I saw a Divine Light shining down on all of us and specially radiating from her.

This was an unbelievable experience and I was not the least bit tired because my "Universe' stepped in and filled me up with this radiant Divine love.

I was going to protect her from anything and anyone until she was grown up and then some. That was a promise that was sacred to me and that could not be broken for anything.
I knew how it was like not to have a Mother and Father and wonder why. I wanted her to have both like the other kids had. I was grateful I had a fantastic Grandfather and Grandmother. Right after giving birth I called my Grandfather and Helga (my Grandmother had passed away when I was 5 or 6) and told them the news. He was so happy and also surprised that I sounded so relaxed and awake and fresh.

I was overjoyed that she was healthy and I knew this one was a strong one and that the love I had for her surpassed everything I had ever felt for anyone. I would protect her with my life.

Having this little wonder so close I felt that I had gotten the best gift in the world and that I was so lucky she was healthy.

Some years passed and it was time for my son to be born. Since I was in this for the long haul I wanted my daughter to have a sibling. It was another amazing experience giving birth to him and it was completely different because this time I was doing this for the second time and I knew what was going on. I knew the miracles of giving birth so I prayed hard that he would be healthy and so he was.

The Divine energy once again filled the room opening up to the 'heavens' and in the middle my son shone like a beam of bright illuminating light. The light was coming from the above and from him and oh how he was radiating this beautiful light and love. It was so beautiful I cried.

Without really understanding it at the time I had accomplished all my Grandfathers wishes. He had mentioned to me that he wanted 2 Great Grandchildren and shortly afterward he left this plain. It was a bittersweet time. My love for my children gave me such a beautiful love. My Grandfathers passing left me realizing that the one person who gave me the greatest gift had gone and he was missed immensely. He was very near me and always making sure I knew it. He would be there in my dreams and making things disappear and making sure the picture of him fell many times so I had to go and pick it up.

The year he passed I was directed to buy angels to put on the Christmas tree. I found angels in all kinds of gold and all kinds of sizes. Was it you?

Of course it was us/him. We wanted you to know you weren't alone.

OMG I felt so empty without him even though I felt he was very near. I was always very near to tears and still today I remember the feeling and now when I am writing this the tears are falling in streams. The love is eternal, but I was not aware of that then.

Year 29.

The years passed and my life with their father deteriorated because of his 'side steps' or you might call it 'side sleeping' and my 'Universe' was seeing my struggle so one evening they stepped in when I was alone in the house listening to Enya and feeling very close to them…

> We were there showing you what your ex husband was doing. You could see in your minds eye what he was up to and then when you thought that you were going crazy because you could see things like that, you got the picture proof. Remember?

Yes, I remember him taking a vacation, without me knowing it. I found out because his Mother said he was not coming home in a week and I needed to pick up the kids from school. I was furious.

> The key to the mailbox was put right in front of you. You went to check the mailbox and he had had some pictures developed and suddenly you saw the physical pictures that you had seen in your minds eye. Remember?

Yes, I had a hard time understanding that it was true and that I had seen them in my minds eye. I was glad that I saw I wasn't going crazy and that I had that 'gift' of seeing again. But I was very hurt and devastated that he would do such a thing to me and our family.

For the younger digital generation I just want you to know this was the time when you had to develop your pictures on film to paper and you sent the rolls to Kodak for development and they would send them back a week later. ☺

He knew he had you at home with the kids and he thought he could behave just like his Dad had done. It was a pattern he had learned and thought nothing of it.

For him that was normal until I put my foot down. I love my freedom therefore I like everybody to be free. I understand that what freedom is to me is not always how the other person sees it. I feel that I let things 'happen' in our relationship and I let things go and did not see clearly even though I sensed a lot, but had a hard time believing what I 'saw'.

Yes we know. You just couldn't believe what was right in front of you and for that reason you started to resent him. We saw that you had to get out of that relationship because it was dragging you down. You started to read Shirley MacLaine's books, remember?

Yes I remember and I remember I loved that she 'was not afraid to tell it like it was'. She did care what people said about her but it didn't stop her from telling her truth. She literally went 'Out on a Limb' about the other worlds and truths she had experienced. I felt a kinship with her because I related to those worlds as well and am grateful that she stood up and enlightened us with what she saw.

He didn't like her and didn't like me reading those kinds of books. He tried to make me feel that I wasn't worth anything and told me I was naive because I believed in good things in all people. Even though I had been through many bad things I always saw the good side and gave people the benefit of the doubt.

Yes you always saw the beauty in people and for you the glass was always half full.

He always saw the negative side of life and I just could not go there. He wanted to make me believe I was not intelligent and that I couldn't amount to anything. I feel that it was good that he did that, it made me more focused and determined to have a life that I wanted to have. Sometimes I felt defeated but 90 % of the time I kept seeking a new life. My children were the factor that kept me grounded and kept me fighting to get to a better place.

Today I can see what he was afraid of. Somewhere he knew even though he felt his family was 'better' than mine he didn't feel worth anything so no one else should either. That kind of thinking was foreign to me. I had this inner belief that life was magical and that I had a possibility to be in that magic and couldn't understand those that were so negative about life. I did have negative streaks when I almost lost my 'faith' but most of the time I was positive about things.

Do you remember the kids sailing?

Yes I do. I introduced them to it.

Do you remember why you did that?

I wanted them to learn a great sport and be part of a positive environment.

Yes but you wanted them to be with people that loved to sail and people who had class and who saw the world beyond the couch. He would always want to be home and sleep and it made you angry.

So you went and spent time with your kids sailing and going to competitions. It was fun for you all.

I wanted them to be able to be with all kinds of people and feel comfortable in yacht races and at beautiful hotels and restaurants and to feel 'at home' whether it was in castles or the local pizzeria.

You wanted your children to be able to be in any part of the world and be confident in their skin.

Yes that is why I globe-trotted the world with them. I wanted them to see this beautiful planet and its people of all cultures. I felt that part of their 'education' was to visit places to understand that people come in all shapes and sizes and from all different kinds of cultures and that we are all part of the same planet.

How did I know to teach them this? I always felt that when my children were born they were independent individuals that I was 'taking care of' until they could take care of themselves. I never felt they were 'my' children, understood that I never felt I owned them, but that they had blessed me with their presence and I was lucky to learn from them. I also felt that I was lucky that they had chosen me to take care of them and honored them as fully capable human beings with their own minds and integrity. I let them have much freedom to explore their world. My only concern was for their safety, other than that they were free to express their true essence. I thank my Grandfather for teaching me this by doing the same for me.

Do you remember being able to see through people?

Yes I do.

Now that I think about it I remember that I did that all the time as a child. I could see things before they happened and I really saw more than most people.

Will I ever be able to see people as clearly as when I was a child? You guys made me remember how I saw it. Oh my God, this is huge.

Soon you will be able to see like you did when you were a child again.

We also see you coming into your own power where you are not letting doubt take over any more. There are still some small bits coming and going but you are handling it very well. You are just letting it go through the heart and then you are letting it go.

There are still some 'leaves falling' and when doubt creeps up it stops you from your development and stops you from seeing. Continue with the work, continue disintegrating negativity or negative thoughts by putting a heart around it and see it dissipate. Continue seeing the truth in everything.

Ok, I see. All I need to do is whenever I feel a lower frequency feeling I surround it with a heart, breathing in and then breathe out with the heart surrounding the feeling and it dissipates. Wow so simple. Where there is love, fear cannot be.

Yes, it IS simple, because there is no vibration that is stronger than the *love* vibration so anything lower than that will dissipate.

Do you remember Mexico?

Yes I do, how could I forget?

You sold everything in Sweden, your house, your car, and all your belongings and you left for Mexico with a ticket and two suitcases and only one of them made it. That's what we call law of non-attachment.

Yes I remember. I had no doubts I just 'jumped of the cliff' literally. Something larger than my-self just took over and I didn't doubt that this was the way.

And when you totally trusted in us, when everybody was telling you that it would be difficult, you said I am going anyway, that was beautiful.

But I already knew I needed to be in this country. I had longed to be here for so long.

Yes, that's true; your Soul had already left. You already knew it. On the other hand it was still beautiful that you totally trusted in us.

First things started to happen. You had gotten divorced and you were in Lund and you said. "I can't stay here. I have to go."

Sweden was over for me. I needed a larger 'stage'. Remember I said in the beginning I knew I would be back in the States...

Your Mother calls you out of the blue and guess what, we were there. We told your Mother and her husband to give you some of their money. They were refinancing the house and taking out some money to enjoy. And they said you know what, we are going to enjoy a little bit and give to our kids.
Guess who put that in their minds?

Hmm that is interesting. Up until that time my Mother had never given me anything monetary prior to that. I know she helped my half-brother and sister so this was a big surprise. But a lovely surprise.

So suddenly you see the money is there and Jonas was going to Mexico and you said "Hey you know what?" "I am going with you." So you went, but before you went, remember you went to this clairvoyant lady? She looked at you when you came in with Caroline and she kept looking at you. She worked with Caroline first and when they were finished Caroline came out and was paying her the 500 kronor. Then she looked at you and when you two sat down she said, "Thank you for visiting me here." You had a puzzled look on your face and was wondering what she meant. She looked at you and she says; "Oh my God, you are so stubborn that your people are having such a hard time getting through to you." You didn't know what she meant.

Well I knew I had a stubborn streak in me but I was puzzled at the way she talked to me.

62

Then she took your hands and she slapped them, "You have got to work with these hands, you have to work with colors, you have to continue doing that, you know this." She was saying things to you and you didn't understand what she meant. She talked to you like you were above her, which puzzled you.

When you were nearing the end of the session you were thinking ok I am going to pay this woman. She looked at you and said, "No, I am not allowed to take any money from you." And you were like, "What?" She says no, "You should be telling me about my life not the other way around."

I remember being in a puzzled state of mind when I left her and wondering what she saw and why she treated me like that. Again I have to say that I see it now and when I look back I understand 'the Universe' having a hard time getting through to me. I see that when I became 'grown up' I felt that I ran my life, nobody else did and I create it as well. I see I was coming from a place of Ego and not the heart like I do now.

Well you have always come from your heart but not 100% like you are now. But your intention has always been through love. That is all you know and that is all you have ever known.

She said: "You are very powerful, you have a great life ahead of you, but you will encounter difficulties if you leave right away for the US." She didn't know how to say it or what to say because she was so perplexed that you had come to her. She could see how powerful you were. She could see what you could see, but she could also see that you were not seeing it or were blind to it.

When you left her place and told Caroline that she would not take any payment, Caroline became jealous.

63

You were still wondering what she meant and so on and so forth. We hope that you understand now what she had seen and what you were able to do in her eyes. You are finally coming to your power the power you have had your whole life. You have just been keeping yourself on a lower vibration.

Do you remember that time you and Caroline meditated and you saw very clearly, who you were going to meet and how he was going to look and that you were going to meet someone. You were not really sure if it was in 'spirit' you would meet him or in the flesh.

You knew exactly what he was going to do. He was going to speak Spanish first and you were going to look at him and think and know he was not from Spain or Mexico and then he was going to go over to speak to you in English/American.

Guess what, that is exactly what happened. Remember what happened when Dennis came over on the beach?

Yes I remember. Well I remember his dog came over first and skutted sand on me while I was trying to meditate. Then I heard someone laughing out loud and then he came over to talk.

He was a little bit bigger and wasn't as pretty as you had seen, but guess what, we were there too. That encounter was NOT coincidence and like we say, nothing is coincidence.

I know and I thank you for introducing me to him. I knew my trip to Mexico that first time was special and life changing and it was.

I had to travel back and forth between Sweden and Mexico to sell all my belongings and then I stayed. I could see that the Mexico I saw as a tourist was not the Mexico I saw as a resident. Life was not easy and soon it was time for another change.

Remember your trip when you two had to flee from Mexico?

Yes.

Because all the 'doors' were closing and you had no way to support yourselves and both of you were looking at each other and thinking ok, we have to get back to the United States.

Remember when you were driving and almost drove over a bicyclist?

Yes I do, how could I forget.

Well we made sure that that didn't happen. He was closer than you thought. Do you remember the car suddenly speeding up?

Yes I do,

That was us.

Oh my God. I couldn't understand why I was speeding up,

Because at that speed you weren't able to stop in time so you had to speed up.

Oh my...

and you hadn't seen the biker.

No, I remember I hadn't but Dennis had.

Yes, exactly that was us. We just put the gas down, because we knew if you had gone your normal speed you would have crashed and you would not have been able to get out of Mexico because the biker would have died.

Wow.

Do you also remember renting the car?

Yes I do.

You did see that the car was gold, remember?

Yes I do. Does that have any significance being gold?

We were wondering when you would ask that. Yes it is a protective color.   You were protected by us and that is why nobody saw you or the car without license plates and you crossed the border with it. Remember?

Oh? Yes I remember thinking that I was 'lucky' and so did Dennis.

You went to the airport in Puerta Vallerta, Mexico to rent a car. You had no plane ticket because you weren't going anywhere by flight. So the first rental company didn't want to talk to you and it wasn't you who was talking to them it was Dennis. He only had a debit card and they didn't take his card. The next rental company Dennis went to didn't want to talk to him either and then he went to the third rental company, but you had gone and listened to everything he had said to these people and so on the fourth one you said, "Ok, that's it, I am taking over." You took over because we had been listening to the stories he had been telling and in your mind we knew that you had to take over, but it was us who took over.

I see you took over because everything went easily and at the time I thought it was too easy. That is the only way I can explain it.

You went with your debit card. You had a Swedish debit card in Mexico and we can tell you that that is impossible to get through, but you had the story down you had everything down.

67

When you rented that car, remember you talked about meeting your Aunt in Guadalajara for Easter. You spoke directly from your heart to her heart. You said you have an Aunt you hadn't seen in a long time that you needed to see for the week of Easter. You said you had a card that was Swedish and it was a debit card and you overpowered her and she could not say anything else but yes. And we were there with you. Do you remember going out to the car and you found out it had no license plates? And you were like, Holy Sh***t there are no license plates!!! This car is so new there are no license plates!! You guys made it across the US Mexican border and you went into the Border Patrol Office in Texas and you knew this car had no license plates and you were thinking, "Oh boy, how is this going to work." You also knew it was a Mexican registered car and you were driving it across the border into the United States and you went and you had no visa going to the States.

Remember the guy at the counter?

Yes.

He called you as soon as you got in the room, you looked around and he pointed at you and says no, "You." Because you were the only blond in there, everybody else was dark and short and you were a head taller than everybody else.

Do you remember you walked in there and the guy looked at you and your passport and said "Yeah that's all right, but you have to be out of the country in 3 months, but you can come in." You walked out completely relieved and thinking oh my, this is fantastic and you left and nobody checked your car, nobody checked your license plates and you got through the boarder and entered Texas and you ended up in Ft Davis.

By this time you and Dennis were pretty tired and hungry. John S 'saves' you by inviting to dinner and you are like oh my God this is wonderful.

The universe was working with you and now you know we were.

Do you remember when you went back up to the camper on top of the mountain to sleep and suddenly torrential rains and hail come out of the sky? The hail were the size of golf balls and you were like Holy Moly, here we have a rental car from Mexico and I am not going to be able to explain to the rental company that we had a hail storm in Guadalajara, let alone explain that we took the car out of the country and crossed the border.

Something took over me and I went into action to 'save the car from possible hail damage' mode.

I could see a future where I was a fugitive 'on the run' with a 'stolen' Mexican registered car and wanted to avoid that. I couldn't have it ruined by hail so I needed to 'save' this car from hail damage and Dennis was screaming what are you doing out in the middle of the storm.

I screamed," I am saving this car covering it with blankets because otherwise the car could be filled with hail marks and I am not going to be able to explain it to the rental company!" "And I don't want to be a run away fugitive with this car!"

You went out there and big hail clumps were falling down almost the size of golf balls. We were protecting you while you went out there and put Mexican blankets over the car. You draped them around the car and closed the doors so the car was safe, and then you come back in.

69

Dennis was really worried that you were going to get yourself killed. But you knew we were with you so you weren't worried. The next day you saw the car was ok even though it was soaking wet on the inside you were thanking us for it, because you were going to have to turn around and get the car back to Mexico. We were with you on all of that. We were also with you when you came back and did your vision quest and asked where you were supposed to go.

Do you remember when you were in Ft. Davis when you had no money and you were praying? Guess what? Suddenly a whole team of bicyclists needed massages at the next ranch and you are a massage therapist, so you went to work full time with that and Dennis got work playing some music. He and you made money. Remember the car you bought?

Yes. It was a red Ford 150 "from the turn of the century" ok no but it was old and Richard sold it to us. It had a bicycle horn and for us to drive it we had to have it inspected on the border of Mexico because that was the only place they would pass it. Come on, the horn was put on the outside mirror. I remember Dennis wanted to park the car in front of a restaurant we were going to and I said, park it in the back where no one can see it. When we started it up it sounded like the car Onslow would drive in the English series 'Keeping up Appearances'. I remember one evening we drove it to a nice place and I had dressed all in white, when I got out of the car I was covered in black spots, and I saw it when I went to wash my hands in the restroom before dinner. I wondered what it was and tried to dust it off. I realized it was all over me and it came from the ceiling of the car. The car broke down 28 days later, while crossing a creek, and we were leaving for DC 2 days later. All we had needed was for the car to 'work' for a month. We needed some money and sold it to good friends of John's. I am sure they bought the car because I needed to sell it, because I heard they never got it to run.

A month later you sold it for a penny less, so suddenly you guys had enough money to get yourselves to Washington DC. Guess who was behind all that?

Ok guys I see what you were saying. You have been with me my whole life and lifetimes back as well. You have been with me all time.

Yes, that is how it is and you don't get rid of us because we stick like crazy glue.

Funny ☺
I remember laughing on top of that mountain when you showed me the Neon Sign that was brilliantly colorful and flashing and it read 'Washington DC' in huge letters. I laughed so hard because there was no doubt; it was crystal clear, what the sign said. Even a blind person would have been able to see that. We had to go to Washington DC.

We made sure Dennis got the job. We were there the whole time.
We have been with you the whole time. Dennis got this job after he lost this job. He got another one and got better and better jobs because we knew you needed to have some security, some economical security. You got a job and you saw how horrible it was and the negativity was almost killing you. Then you got the job with BGR that almost killed you. We took you out before it killed you and then that's when Sai Maa Lakshmi Devi steps in. You saw that this kind of life, this rat race is not for you, you were not made for it. When Sai Maa comes in, you were back on the spiritual path.

I am seeing my path in front of me much clearer than I remember ever doing.

71

You see much clearer because you have been through a lot in life and have come out on the other side and understand where you have been and know why you are here on Earth. You know your mission, you have remembered why you are here and what you as a Soul decided to do before coming down.

So we cannot stop you, even if we wanted to. That's a train that you jumped on before you even came down on this earth. That is what your Soul decided before you came to Earth.

So I am still under construction, or in other words you guys are still working on me?

Oh yes, we are still working on you and we will continue doing this and that's why you feel the headaches when you wake up and during the day because you are feeling the high energy vibration.

Yes I do feel it.

Well, we are trying to do what it takes people a lifetime to accomplish, and we are doing it in a very short time. But you are responding very well to it.

I appreciate all you are doing for me and with me. I cannot even begin to tell you how grateful I am for having you on this journey.

We are grateful that you remembered because if you didn't we would not be on this wonderful journey with you and telling it to the world. We are grateful that you have not wavered to finish this even though it has been daunting at times.

If I was able to see what I saw when I was a child then I must have been up on a higher level and completely open. Was I up on higher frequencies as a child?

Yes. You were up on the higher frequencies a lot.

Was I up on higher frequencies than I am now?

Yes, but not all the time, but you were up there a lot and you were very open and loving. It was natural for you to be there and it was play for you and you were up there all the time.

Was I in the light?

Yes, and that is what your name means. You were in the flow. You were in the state of *one*, meaning you were one with the trees, the birds, the sky, the sun, the Universe.

Am I going to be in that state again?

Yes, that is the state all 'enlightened masters' talk about when you are *one with all*. You will come back to that state and you are there you just don't know it yet. There are still some shedding left to do. And that is what we are helping you with.

So all you guys are doing is taking all this crap that I have accumulated on myself while being down in this physical form and now you are fine tuning me and removing it from me?

Yes that's a good way of putting it. That is what we are doing.

Wow.

You liked being up there, you could put yourself up there in no time. You just walked down the path to the river at your Grandfather's place and you were there. That's why nothing ever happened to you. You were *one with everything*. That's why you were never scared and you are also feeling right now that the fear is going away. You are not resonating with fear anymore. People around you are still having the fear.

I am going to make an attempt to explain how fear really messes it up for us. Fear keeps us in a vegetative state, it is the cause of most sicknesses like depression and it keeps us procrastinating. It really keeps us in a state of 'paralysis' regarding our life. Fear keeps us in a state of 'standby mode' instead of a 'living a full life mode'. When I realized that my 'stagnation' was caused by fear I was surprised because I had never seen it like that. The interesting part of fear is that it is the opposite of love. It is not a natural state to be in. When we are born we don't have fear in us, we are 100% love and radiate it. Fear is a learned state and I wish I never had to learn it. I also see that without fear I wouldn't know what love is so I guess it served its purpose. From now on I have decided to only radiate love.

Whenever Dennis says negative things to you in front of your son, he does it because he is trying to get your vibration down because he sees you are flying. He has gotten to a higher vibration because of Sai Maa, but he knows he won't be able to reach you, and it makes him uneasy.

He sees you soaring so high so he tries to get you down on a lower level. He is not doing it on purpose it's something he doesn't think he is doing, but he is doing it because of fear. He also sees you are strengthening your relationship with your son. Your son can't stop your positive love energy, he enjoys it. He is enjoying being around your love. He thinks it's a fun time and you know it. You love having him around and Dennis has seen that and is a bit jealous about that. You are giving your son a little bit of a hard time with a twinkle in your eye and always with a smile and he loves it. Whenever you come out from your room your son is coming out too because he loves that energy you give. He doesn't know why but he loves it.

Yes, I am enjoying myself with him. I feel I am powerful again and can joke with him and he sees I have regained my power and he likes it. I believe that is why he is leaving now. Of course it has to do with his evolvement as well but he sees I am strong again and he needs to live his life his way.

We see that and we are very happy for you and we know that touches your heart very deeply because you know you have hurt him through the divorce. You are making up for it very much right now. Just continue working with yourself and your beautiful energy and your beautiful book.

Oh yes my dears, I would never stop even though I know this book is probably going to get my other family mad.

Yes and no because you are going to put a spin on it so they understand, you are not mad at them you just need to tell your story so you can help the world. Your mother will cry when she reads this because she feels she will be exposed but she will have to understand that this is your path and you have to do this for a higher purpose.

Yes, I know.

Someone wrote this – "You own everything that happens to you. Tell your stories. If people wanted you to write warmly about them, they would have behaved better."

> And your brother will be mad at you but he will also see what's behind. He will also see you are not out there to 'leave' your Mother out there but that it is something that has happened. You know what goes around comes around. They will be hurt but your love will shine through and they will understand it even though it will hurt them initially.

Dear Readers, This was directed to my 'Universe' in the beginning of me writing this book.

"I want people on Earth to wake up so that we don't ruin our planet. I want them to be connected with Mother Earth. I feel she is our mother. I want people to wake up and smell the trees, feel the breeze, enjoy the sun and the stars but to feel at home here on Earth and to love her. That's what I want because Mother Earth loves us back and that's what I envision with this book. By creating love all around people, they will be able to give love to the earth to their families and to send away fear.

I want our awakening to be that our DNA comes back in the form that it was when we were multi dimensional beings. We were Divine and we lived in love. Now if that's a utopia and that is something that has never happened and something only in fairytale books well then let me know. I know what happens when I send out love and people feel the love they send it on many times more. That's what I want to be happening. I just want to show them the way of love. Now am I able to do that? Is that the way of this book? "

> YES. We love this. This is what you are doing with your book. You are showing by example.

Love Not GMO.

People today are very unhappy and living in fear. They don't see any hope of things getting better. They are disillusioned and bitter. Many have turned away from the Church because they don't resonate with the message given to them anymore. There are so many rules to follow that people have lost hope. There is this undertone of despair, and it is quite dark. Many people will want to leave this planet because they don't see any hope for it getting better.

Will this book help them? Will they believe in it?

Yes, that is what we are talking about. We see this book taking them to a new level of hope and joy. With this book you will open up the eyes of people and open up their hearts and help them see that they CAN do something about their lives and their children's lives.

It is quite a large task you are putting on me. I am not sure I still understand what I am to do. I feel there are so many 'book promoters' out there and I don't want to be another one.

> We understand and you are not a book promoter you are a genuine leader of love with a mission of enlightenment for the masses.

How will I make a difference?

> By showing how to live in love and in integrity. You are the 'way-shower' and you will lead by example. We are seeing a growing hostility towards governments and religious institutions and many things and old school thinking and government that don't work anymore. We do not want you to be worried. Just dance around it and spread the love.

Ok?

> The reason we are speaking to you is for you to be able to be forewarned about the happenings in the making. You are going to go on a tour around the states and see for yourself what is happening to your fellow countrymen/women. You got a little peek yesterday with Cindy but now as soon as this book is finished we will show you the ramifications of what Monsanto and DuPont and other chemical companies have done and you will see the devastation, but you will be able to help these people who have lost hope. They are losing their farms and their ability to sustain their families and it is looking much like it did in the 1920's

> We see violence is going to increase and we want you to send hearts to the places before you go there.

When you get there your message will be a breath of fresh air but the people will be skeptical at first. They will understand that they have nothing to lose and with your grace they will listen and do what you say in order for them to turn their farms around.

The sun is spreading its love frequency everyday ☺

When you talk about GMO you are talking about putting hearts around the crops and sealing them from the GMO.

Your hearts around your crops destroy the GMOs and then after wards you envelope the soil in hearts and you 'cleanse' your soil. When you plant with your heirloom natural seeds you also envelope them in hearts and do it with your tractor as well. Make sure your whole property is enveloped in a huge heart bubble everyday and do it with your family and friends.

After a while you will notice a larger crop harvest and also a healthier crop. Keep surrounding your property with a huge heart bubble and you will see results. Of course you have to water and use organic fertilizer and when it is time to harvest, the GMO seeds that have come upon your property, will not survive they will be destroyed by the heart frequency. Sometimes if the farmer has a lot of doubt it will take longer like the second harvest will be successful, but all will succeed if you follow these simple steps. Imagine your family enveloped with a huge heart every day. The same way you say Good Morning to your family members you surround each one with a heart and you will see how fast the ship will be turned around. The reason the GMO crops cannot survive is because the crops are a construct and the frequency is lower than the frequency of the heart. This is something that will spread like the sun spreads her rays in the morning.

The most important thing to do in the morning is to surround your property and everyone on the farm/ranch/property with hearts. If you have plants that are sick just surround them with hearts and of course tend to them with natural means and see what happens. Helene was doing this while she was writing this book and was amazed at the result.

We see the future of Big Pharma, GMO manufacturers, Governments and Institutions that are not working for the good of the people failing. These corporations will be exposed because their interests do not serve the people. People will silently surround their families and crops with hearts and get rid of unwanted effects that have happened because of the GMO crops. The effects will be seen through people getting rid of their sicknesses due to ingesting the GMO processed foods.

They will start taking back their health by eating non-GMO food and fertilizing their farms organically and living in the highest vibration of love.

We like that you are starting to understand that the GMO crops cannot be a 'fight against anything' it's a 'LOVE on the things'. 'Fighting against anything' means you are just going into their agenda and that is being on their lower vibration. So when people collectively surround their property and their families and their crops and their cities and countries with hearts, then they take back their lives and their power.

To change anything there is only one vibration that works and that is the LOVE vibration. If people want to change their Governments, Banks, Churches and Countries then they have the tools to do this. They no longer are helpless but can do this by sending hearts to resolve conflicts and 'cure' corruption.

So people have the power in their hearts and when they use this power collectively they 'rule'. They can turn hurricanes around purely by sending hearts to the area. I was not here in this country at the time but was told that it was done in the 1970's through a radio program called Coast to Coast with the host and 2 million listeners and they turned a storm in the Carolinas around.

People are raising their frequencies and ascending together with Mother Earth and understanding the heart connection that changes lives.

I believe so.

Let's look at this again. We are seeing people awakening to their true potential by opening their hearts. When people gather and help each other and join hearts then 'miracles' happen. The *love* on things you want to change is the key to being successful.

81

If you fight against anything you go against the flow, which is going against nature, and it gets you nowhere. To have the 'help' from the Gods/Universe you have to be in 'the Flow' and only then does it become successful. Being 'in the flow' is being in the highest vibration of love.

Wow that is profound.

Yes, hearts destroy GMO and when people gather and send hearts to troubled areas, conflicts get resolved and corruption ceases to exist. Can you see how powerful you are? And it is all done through love, isn't that a beautiful way to resolve conflicts?

Yes I love it. I have been using it with all of my conflicts in my everyday life and it works. I noticed if someone was mad at me I would send hearts and surround the people and issues with hearts and they would be resolved very fast. It is amazing and works!

So that is partially the story and then the tools to become enlightened and the tools to succeed is love in what you do, say and are. The tools people take away from the book is that love conquers, love heals and love connects.

I am amazed at how fast it works.

Yes and we see you are 'seeing a room full of men', like farmers and ranchers, that are not going to be taking this seriously. Like you know when there is any success, it's because the wives get together and they see the whole picture. To be successful you will target the women first and then the men will wake up.

Ok, so what about all these scenes that I saw in the beginning of writing this book? I saw people in large gatherings at community centers and farmers harvesting their crops.

Your book has evolved.

Does it mean I leave it out?

No you will include it. That is a vital part for the farmers who want to take back the control of their farms from the Monsanto GMO crops. They will be looking at that chapter more, but they will also be getting your story behind it all and how you came upon this.

Ok.

So we recommend you continue writing your story from your heart and when you are in that space that is what they will be getting. We will be guiding you the same time you are writing.

I just got off the phone with Cindy regarding her cows. She told me that she had to let two cows go because they had become infertile from eating GM Genetically Modified hay. Their hormones went off balance after they had eaten the GM hay which may also have been fertilized with synthetic fertilizers.

The place she used to get her hay from had run out and she was out of hay herself so she went to an other farmer who guaranteed her that his hay was not GMO. After the cows had eaten it she noticed they acted differently and so she suspected something was not right. She told me that at her Fathers farm they didn't have those kinds of problems.

She said "in those days her Father didn't have to take care of his animals like she has to" because they didn't have the synthetics they have today. She nurses her farm animals like babies and this loss was devastating to her. She mentioned that she believes some of the farmers get kickbacks to grow the GMO crops.

What many are awakening to and seeing are the GMO's devastating effects on people and livestock. Many more farmers/ranchers have these problems and there is a way to change this and that is what this book will help show.

People have the power to destroy GMO by surrounding them with hearts.

The farmers are able to plant their crops without any fear of GMO because they will be planting with hearts surrounding each plant or seed. The GM seed will eventually die out destroying itself from the inside. This fear that has been caused by the companies will not be sustainable because the farmers will conquer it with their love, which is stronger than anything in the world and Mother Earth protects these individuals.
People see the connection and start to treat Mother Earth as a precious being who belong in their hearts and who takes care of them and who is more important than any economic plan or scheme that other interests are trying to achieve. The 'other' interests will be exposed with all of the rest of the 'plans' that are in place to control people and people will see this clearly and not tolerate it any more. Consciousness is rising and people will not stay in the dark, they will evolve and wake up.

When people imagine the heart and surround the seed or plant with it and plant it in the soil it will cleanse Mother Earth, it will cleanse her streams, trees, plants and water. When every plant is planted with Love people will be *one* with the plants. Plants will be *one* with you/them.   This will also make the plants grow bigger and healthier. By surrounding seeds and plants and property with hearts, not only will the plants grow healthier they will reprogram the cells which are resistant to GMO so the GMO will not survive. Love is stronger and it will destroy GMO.

People believe you because you talk through your heart to their hearts.

I am seeing a pasture with all these hearts.
How do I do it? How do I do it with my plants?
How will I teach this?

You will go out and surround each one of your plants with a big huge heart. Every day you will surround your property with a huge heart. You will walk all around the property and it is just like sage-ing but with a heart. You will surround plants and animals with hearts. Just imagine a big huge red heart bubble around every plant, grass, animal, and person you meet.
Imagine the whole Earth filled with hearts! You will be going to schools teaching kids how to plant with hearts.

When I meet policemen or see a police-car I surround the car or police with a heart? Right?

Yes, that is how you do this.

I can see and imagine the place with hearts, like a field with hearts exactly like the pictures I am envisioning.

When people imagine these hearts in their minds they will realize their power. It starts with one seed and spreads and germinates to the others and multiplies.

The key ingredient here is *love*.

Love conquers fear, love is stronger and love will spread along with the planting of the seeds. When the plants have 'grown' the people will eat these plants with the high frequency of love and they will get that *love* inside them. This is not only the fountain of health, because when you eat food with the frequency of love, sicknesses cease to develop, it is the real fountain of youth. When you eat food that is planted with love and surrounded with love and you have surrounded your property with love, this 'love' envelopes everything and it rejuvenates your blood cells.

Imagine the blood cells looking like little hearts and they pass through your whole body. This is the ultimate fountain of youth because your cells get that very high vibration and that high vibration is *love* which gives life. It is contagious and soon everybody will be smitten with love.

See your veins filled with hearts…

Can you imagine what will happen when everybody will be 'smitten' with love?

Wow, what a beautiful 'revelation'.

In religion and theology, revelation is the revealing or disclosing of some form of truth or knowledge through communication with a deity or other supernatural entity or entities.

Yes exactly. Isn't it wonderful and all it is, is *love*. Love will silently work its way through peoples' food and change them from the inside. Isn't this just beautiful?

Yes, I almost can't believe it has not 'worked' yet or that nobody has done this yet.

Well you do remember the 60's and 70's love revolution.

Yes I do. Well I was young then but I have read about it.

The Governments didn't want the 'wave' of the love revolution to succeed so wars were designed to keep people in fear, of course one shouldn't forget the money that was made on wars as well. Too many people were turning to love and that was seen as dangerous for the 'powers to be'. When there is *love*, fear cannot rule. In order to keep the power they needed to control what was happening and then the drugs were spread to make sure that the pure love that was flowing would cease. You see, the 'powers to be' knew that when people went into the love energy, they would see that they had the power within themselves and could not be controlled.

To keep the status quo and not lose control they had to create disasters and wars and drugs to keep people in fear and ignorance.

It is so obvious that I could scream but that would not do any good so I will write and hopefully more and more people will wake up to this.

It is a very fine line and if you look at how the manipulation has been going on for so long you will see that time and time again when people start getting powerful in themselves then new 'fear' related events suddenly happen out of thin air.

Powerful countries create wars to get people to stay in fear and the news broadcasts (paid for by the powers to be) survive on fear and so on. So your idea of not having a TV is great and like you saw, many of your friends don't have them either. Gradually people are really seeing what TV does and they have seen through the lies and don't want to be part of it anymore.
This has been going on for eons and is not a new phenomenon but now you see it and your mission is to silently spread the love through healthy love plants and restore the love and health in people. By doing this you will simply create a silent Love Revolution.

You will go to some of the farms and you will take the shovel and the seed and put a heart around the seed in your minds' eye and with hands put the seed in the ground and put earth over and water. You will see the heart and seed grow together. When the seed grows the heart grows bigger around it. Put a heart around the sack of seeds. Surround the tractor with a huge heart. Surround the whole property with a huge heart before planting seeds. The heart penetrates and surrounds the property all the way to the center of the earth and all the way out to the Universe.

Stand in the middle of your property and surround it with the heart bubble and then soak it in love all around. Get yourself on the property infused with a heart and the tractor too. Imagine a bright red shiny big fat and beautiful heart incasing Mother Earth, while you are at it.

Wow I see this.

You see a huge heart surrounding the earth and water. When letting water out of the faucet you see hearts coming out. The place where you live is inside a huge heart.

When you greet people who come to these meetings you shake their hands and they will instantly be having that heart energy go throughout their systems, which will turn on their lights and they will get it. All you have to do is show the slides and demonstrate how to do it.

When you speak and people 'get it' and want to do it right away give them some business cards or t-shirts to help keep them motivated. You will start with the school kids and they will tell their parents and before you know it, more people will be touched by this revelation.

The communities will start seeing that they should not be spraying chemicals on the ground and a lot of things will be changing. When people wake up they will feel their hearts grow and what started as growing the garden with love they will be feeling with their loved ones and towards their friends and everyone they meet. The connection through their hearts will be the key.

The food chains will change and people will celebrate through helping each other more. We will give *love* when we exchange money. Like Jane said we will be handing each other *Love* every time we meet and greet.

I see a field with many small hearts the crop is not large but seems happy. There is a huge heart formed like a balloon all over the property it grows almost like a protective shield over the property. Is that what you are saying?

Yes.

My three grandchildren in a heart bubble:)

I see children running on the property and the hearts are being dropped all over from them.

That is what we see as well.

I am looking to you for the answers. When I touch people or I shake hands with people the love will go into their bodies.

When they plant, the heart that went into their bodies is with them because I have given it to them and it will go into the plant. So I need to touch all who come and then when they touch the crops they will be filling them with hearts and when they harvest the crops the machines will have hearts surrounding them and so on. My books will have the love frequency and when they read the books they will get the hearts inside of them. When they talk the hearts will jump out from them.

When I am in the airplane I will charge the properties with love. I will be sending hearts down on these properties and the wind will take them and spread it around.

How will they believe this?

> They need to feel it in their hearts, they need to learn to visualize in front of them and then spread it all over the place.

It is that simple?

How can people destroy GMO?

> GMO is a construct and all constructs can be taken down by love. Love is your answer.

It seems so simple.

> It *IS* simple. You surround the seeds, the plants, the property, and the people with hearts.

And only the good heirloom seeds will function but the GM seeds will self destruct.

What about the farmers that have bought a lot of the GM seeds and they have them on their farm?

They will be able to put a heart around their property and the seeds will self-destruct.

What about all the money they have put in?

They will need to change their seeds. They will need to take care of their soil.

They will need to surround their soil with hearts, surround their kids, house, property, tractor and their animals with hearts. When they do that their soil will become fertile, their crops will grow and they will become healthier. They will destroy the pesticides by surrounding it with hearts.

So this is the best part of it all, I am looking at the flowers out there on my porch, and see they are doing well this year. Since I started writing this book I have followed your recommendations and every day I have surrounded my loved ones, my animals and home and property with hearts and I see how my plants have really taken off and grown very big compared to last year. I show people by example that it works.

Here is my sun-heart spreading hearts all around.

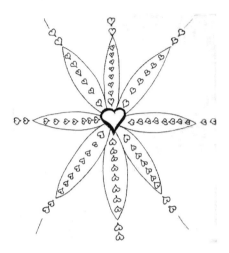

The sun is sending off rays of love. The sun is shining with hearts of rays coming down on all on earth. That's what's happening right now. That is why it is important to be in the sun to stay healthy, contrary to what the establishment has been saying. We all need to soak up the suns' rays to stay healthy.

The suns' rays help the body maintain balance and nourish you so you are able to absorb the minerals and vitamins you need. Of course don't stay in the sun for hours but at least 30 minutes a day and noon is the best time.

That is interesting and against what the conventional doctors are recommending. This will be met with resistance by many people. I have never believed the establishment because I have always seen the truth behind all of these so called dangers. I believe in living in a 'common sense' kind of way and I live with what works for me. If I am not in the sun I feel depleted and my chakras don't spin as well. So I do what feels right for me.

I hope this book will help people see clearly. Again this book is reflecting what I personally believe since I am no doctor I just recommend people using common sense. The plants need the sun to grow and so do we ☺

You will see that people are waking up and your book is coming at the right time. Just in time for the tipping point to happen ☺

I hope so. I feel I will be questioned about many of the subjects in this book.

You will be going to many different places and people will be questioning, but they will not question after they have met you. The news of what you are doing is going to go worldwide and when they see you and they feel you, they will slowly gradually understand what your mission is. You will have the help from all the Ascended Masters and people who have gone over to the other side and a lot of people on this side will immediately understand and start to practice this new 'method of love'.

Just look at this: You give people love and you plant love with every plant. Imagine when everybody is doing this. Everybody can imagine a heart.

Whenever you put a heart bubble around every plant or tree or shrub, you are giving it the love it needs, which is the basics a plant needs to grow. Yes you will be watering it and making sure it has what it needs. Of course you will be doing that, and for the people in Africa that have sand to grow on, you just continue giving them hearts and show them how you do. You will also guide them to create sustainable growing methods like PermaCulture and Food Forests and Water conservation like Jordan already has had success with.

Continue giving the planet and the whole continent hearts. Keep on giving love and encouragement and you let the rest be up to us because Mother Earth is changing. Her climate is changing, yes Global Warming is happening, but not like you hear about in the news, Global Cooling will happen too, it's just part of the cycle. There will be a change of weather patterns and where people will be planting hearts, people will be getting rain too, so that is also a huge part of your mission. You are going to come to these people, you are going to show them how, you are going to touch them and by your words you are going to speak to their hearts and by your heart connecting with their hearts they are going to be radiating this frequency and when they plant a plant they will be planting it with their hearts. The heart frequency will go into the plants' cells and make the plant much stronger. We mean the plant will be GMO resistant. As long as it has the heart surrounding it, it is going to be fine.   And by planting these hearts you are planting a revolution, but a quiet, loving, peaceful revolution.   There will not be a lot of words, or bureaucracy you will have to go through.   You are just going to put hearts around everything. That sounds simple right?   You will put hearts around everything and we are behind you. You will be working on the physical, we will be taking care of the spiritual, and the reason we made it so simple, is because it will not hurt anybody's religion or political beliefs. Everybody talks about love but you are going to go in there with hearts and there is not anybody who can stop you. That is the most powerful weapon we have in the world. We can call it anything we want in the world, but it is the most powerful 'weapon' we have and that is the reason why we are using it.

When people get to feel that unconditional love, they will understand that there *IS* something more than what you see with your two eyes. That is the difference, so *dear one*; you will be making a difference. Your work is going to affect all beings on this planet. You will be working with the whole world. As soon as you are finished with the book you will see the ripple effect start.

95

Once the ripple effect has taken place, you will be seeing where this is all heading. We want you to know that we have been working with this for lifetimes and you will not fail. You will succeed. You just have to be you, this very strong willed loving person that you were born to be. You chose life but you also chose this magnificent life. And that is what you are having. Your life has just taken a turn for the much better.

I will need the help from all people of the world to turn this 'ship' around, right?

Yes you do but you have to show the way first. You have to live the life and Be the change. It is important in all of this that you never forget your roots, never forget where you have been, what you have done, the trials and tribulations you have gone through. Never forget it because it's part of you. But you trusted in us when you went to Mexico, and when you had nothing you trusted in us. And that is one of the reasons we know we can trust in you, because when you had it like you had it, it was pretty bad.

I agree.

Direct Messages Channeled from Source.

"We want you all to hear what we have to say, we are standing here in front of you and we have a message of love for each and every one of you. We will be telling you something that is very important for the survival of Mother Earth and all we are asking you to do is sit and listen. We want you to know that we are here because of your survival and your happiness and your prosperity and your freedom. This is something that we have been planning for a long time. This is something that you have needed for a long time. We are the Star seeds from other galaxies that have seen what has been happening in this world and we have decided to come and help you take care of this for the benefit of everyone on Earth. All we ask is that you listen and follow what we say with love and peace in mind. We are here to help you take back your agriculture, your freedom and your rights.

If you follow what we say you, your family, your neighbors, and your communities will prosper and will once again be able to sustain yourselves in love and harmony and peace. This is something for each and every one of you. This is something that we have been planning for a while, and this is something Helene Vibeke Gross is here as a speaker of. She has kindly relaxed and let us come through her so that you get this message. We see you in peace, with freedom and able to grow your healthy crops. We see you sharing love through your crops and through your communities. We are so happy and pleased that you are here today and that you are giving this a chance because before you know it, this is going to be spreading all over the world. This love and peace message is not only for the United States, it is for the rest of the world.

It is the recipe on how to farm and grow crops that will be healthy for your family, for your neighbors, for your communities for your world. It will help with famine, it will help people that have no bread for their children, it will help them feed their children and their mothers and grandmothers and communities and states and nations. We will be going back to giving to everyone and when you are finished with this meeting please go out and tell every single one of your friends your family and your community. This will spread like fire but this is love, this is brought to you by love. When you tell someone else, you are actually telling them that you love them. So that is the message we have for you and it is very important that you understand that all you have to do is take this one seed, touch it, and imagine a heart around it, and when you put it in the ground all you have to do is envelope it in the heart. This means when you put the seed in the ground you imagine the heart surrounding it and also surrounding the area you plant in. When you are finished planting on your property, before leaving you imagine a huge rounded heart surrounding all the way to the center of the earth and above your whole property. Imagine your property inside a balloon shaped heart and then you just let it go, and wherever you go hearts will follow.

When you touch peoples hands you are giving them your heart. If you can imagine that...then you know exactly what we are talking about. We will be here to help you, so you will be able to fulfill this. Leave the doubt at the doorstep do not take doubt with you.

This is a journey that will be world revolutionizing the way we think, the way we act and the way we are. This book and these t-shirts are just reminders of what you already know; you are already these wonderful beautiful loving people. We are here to remind you to open up your heart and when you leave this meeting you will be feeling much lighter and happier, filled with love, and that love will be passed onto everybody who comes close to you. Everybody you talk to will be feeling this love. Everybody you meet or talk on the phone with will be feeling this love.

The way to make this really powerful and spread it is by helping Helene V. Gross set up meetings like this all over the country, all over the world. If you have a way of helping her spread this message and you know someone that knows another community where she can come and spread this information and this *love* please give her this information. She is going to take this information and spread this beautiful message of love and help the world. Before you know it the whole nation is going to be filled with hearts. Guess what happens to the crime rate? Guess what happens to poverty? It will just be a bad memory. It is possible in this era to do this and we are doing this and you who are here in front of Helene V. Gross will be helping her fulfill this mission. We are eternally grateful that you showed up today and we will be here to help you get this out to the rest of the communities, to your neighbors, friends, family, loved ones and people you love less, hehe but the message is for peace. Who does not want that? We send our love to you, you will feel it when you get up in the mornings you will look over the fields and you will see your crops growing and in your minds' eye you will have hearts around each one of these crops.

When the crops are small the hearts are small when the crops grow big the hearts grow big. When it's time to harvest, the machine you harvest with is going to have a heart around it. It is going to be harvesting with love when you are sitting on top of the harvesting machine, you are going to be filled with love. It is going to be radiating love all over the property.

When you harvest and turn the soil, the soil will be fertilized with hearts. Do not forget that your love is stronger than anything and by spreading your love you are helping sustain your farm and your family.

Now you may be thinking what about the GMO's and how is that going to be? That is just fear-based thoughts which can be won over by love, nothing negative like GMO can survive the vibration of *love*. Love is stronger than the genetically modified seeds. They will self-destruct. There are sciences already saying that the GMO crops have already shown to need more pesticides to be able to grow. The crops do not grow as well and people are starting to wake up to the fact that this GMO is just a very bad construct.

How can you protect your property from GMO evading your property?

You engulf your property in a huge heart that goes from the center of the Earth all the way above your property. You just put that heart all over and around and it will take care of your crops. And GMO seeds that come into your property will self destruct; they will not be able to continue to grow. Your love-hearts are so much stronger and they will reign. We will oversee each and every one of you that takes this to their hearts and we will help you in getting back your property, your freedom, your love, your divinity.

With love comes a new respect for Mother Earth and a new understanding of how she functions. There is a fast growing community that are by the name of 'PermaCulture' who are showing sustainable ways of farming and who are showing how to live in abundance by using these principles.

They create Food Forests' that continue to grow and produce year after year and they teach how to conserve water even in dry Texas. Please look into that. Helene V Gross has been studying this and is using some of these principles and is just in the beginning stages so she is no expert but can see the beauty and simplicity of life unlike the average farmer who is constantly spraying his crops with dangerous pesticides and other unhealthy alternatives and not reaping the benefits like the PermaCulture farmers.

We are looking forward to getting this out to the world and we want you to know that there is nothing and no one who can stop you when you go in love. Your hearts will be so large that whoever is going to try, is not going to have a chance. You are going to stand together and you are going to be united in love and whoever is going to try to stop you is not having a chance because love is more powerful than fear and hate. So please understand that whatever obstacles you will come up against, your love will rule, which means your love will conquer. Love will rise and hate and fear have no chance. There are those who doubt that this can even happen and we just want to say that whatever you doubt is fine, but keep your eyes open and ears open and your *hearts* open.

When your hearts are open to this you will see, you will feel, you will hear that we do make a difference and when I say we, I mean the whole world. We are here to work with you because we are a part of you. Now Helene V. Gross is going to need your help, she is going to need your feedback. Of course you are going to water your plants like you do. But because you love this earth you are not going to fill it with pesticides, unless they are natural. That is all we say.
So please, when you stop buying the pesticides that are not natural, one thing you will be doing too is putting these big chemical companies out of business.

When you grow your crops with love and you eat your crops and you share your crops with each other and your neighbor and you have not fertilized it with anything made synthetically, you will restore Mother Earth back to her natural state and Mother Earth will love you back. The love that you show her, will love you back. She will change her paths so you will have more even crops, because you can create that by the love. Your love for Mother Earth and for your property, will be able to sustain you and if you have any fertilizer or anything like that that you see is not beneficial to your crops, please do not use it. Dispose of it in a way or in a place where all the toxic waste is and we will help you deal with that. Put hearts around it, even the places where you throw your waste put hearts around it, give it your love.

Hearts surrounding flowers

As you do that you will see what will happen with Mother Earth. Mother Earth is changing and her people are changing which is just a normal natural process. The global warming that people have been talking about is something that has happened before and it is something that we do not have to fear. The earth will always change and that is just her way of being, she is in this cycle at the moment and in 26000 years she will go through it again. Just like people change so does Mother Earth.

So the global warming is just another way to get people to live in fear. Change that to live in love. If you only live in love, or we can say, when you only live in love, love for your property, love for your animals, love for your neighbors, love for your family, love for your community love for your country love for your world, You will see what will happen. It will be a huge shift and a huge change, your communities will grow, and your families will grow healthy. When you start eating your plants that you have grown with love, that have grown on property filled with love and you buy fruits and vegetables from your neighbors that have grown their crops with love. You are not going to need the pharmaceutical companies anymore. You are not going to need the pills that you are taking every day. You are going to be free from medicine because your body is going to be in a state of love, which will take care of any illnesses. Did you know that if you feed your body with the right food your body uses this to restore your health? Your body is always trying to get back to the 'blueprint' you were born with which is your healthy body. Your doctors are not going to allow you to just get off your medicine, be reasonable, be responsible but know in your hearts that you can get off any medicine. Know in your hearts that your body will react to this love you are eating from your locally grown farmers that have grown with love. Know that your bodies will react and they will go back to health. One of the main reasons that there are any sicknesses around is because we have been living in fear for such a long time and we have been eating processed foods instead of 'living foods'. It is time to change our lives to live in love! You ask how? This is the way, you envelop yourself in a big heart, and you let that heart go in to all your cells.

Just put that heart around you as if you are standing inside that heart and just let it consume you. It even helps with rejuvenating your cells. It is very powerful. The air that you breathe is love air, so every time you breathe in, just fill your whole body with love. When you breathe out, you breathe out love.

This is something that is going to become second nature to you. Whenever you have an illness just let the heart come in just fill that area, just fill each one of the cells with this. And when you are done with that, you send it to your neighbors you send it to your father, your mother, your kids, your dogs just send this love to everyone. If you live in love, you will be healthy. Send hearts to the people that live in nursing homes, send them all the love you can. Every morning when you get up, send them hearts, every single one of them. Send them your smile, send them your laughter, send them your love, and dance in love. Let the kids play around and jump and do everything.   In the schools send them love, send them love, send them ALL love. You will see if you just touch one person and that person gets it, and gets that dose of love, how this person will flower.

Do you see? Do you see the hearts surrounding the world? Do you see the love spreading? Do you see people smiling?

I plant with love
I live in love
I am love

These are the new terms to live by.

Declare…I am love!

Then envelope yourself with a huge heart,
Just let it consume you.
What we mean by that is, let it go into every single cell.
Let that heart go in and love you, every single cell, until you can
feel, hear, think and see every blood cell as a little heart. See it
running and dancing around all over your cells through your
veins through everything. Your body is being rejuvenated by
the hearts. When you open your eyes all you see is hearts all
around you. When you speak all you see is hearts coming out
of you and you breathe in hearts. You see them in your
bloodstream. Every single blood cell is a little heart. If some of
the blood cells are not up to par these hearts cells will circle
them and infuse all with the hearts.

Right now Helene V. Gross is imagining her head is a heart
with a big smile.

My head in a heart…

This is the way to see yourself, with love. When she walks on properties she is just sending out that love to everyone. Everyone, every rock, every tree, every piece of soil, every grass, and every leaf is love and from Helene all is engulfed in hearts. Everyone can do this.

We are telling you and the rest of the world that by doing this you (all of you) are cleaning up all the pollution. By spreading your hearts and by spreading your love, you are cleaning up the corruption. Everything will be surfacing and all the corruption going on behind closed doors will be exposed in the light. By spreading love, people will awaken to their true nature, which is love.

This is a very good way to spread the message, to spread the message of love.

All institutions around the world that are open to love will embrace it. That is the shift of humanity that is going on. That is the shift that will turn the evil, the hatred, the wars, the money schemes, and money games, it will turn it so that everybody will have food and love, and be taken care of. That is what the shift is about.

And we are starting in 2012. 2020 is about the time when it should really be planted across this world and there are a lot of starships and people from other galaxies that have come here to make sure that this happens. Earth will prevail, and people will be highly evolved, because when you live in love you are an evolved being and that is what is needed in this world. So just take that heart and let it surround you on all dimensions, let it consume you.

When you step into that heart just let it cover you, consume you and just sleep with that heart. Every night when you go to bed, imagine a huge heart and just crawl into that heart. Do the same with your children; visualize a heart around your children's cribs, on your children's beds, around the whole house around your whole property. Just do this all the time.

When you drive your car, put it in a heart, when you meet a cop put a heart around him and his car. When you go to the grocery store and you look at someone, just put a heart around them, put a heart around the whole grocery store. Just continue spreading the love and the hearts, they won't know it but they will feel it. And when they 'awaken', they will start doing the same to other people, and once we do this every single day the ripple effect across the oceans and across the worlds are going to be profound and you will start to see the beauty in all. You are going to see how and what this shift is all about. You will experience what 'The Golden Age' is all about while you are still on Earth. You do not have to go anywhere to be in heaven. We will have it right here.

This concludes today's session with love from the bottom and the top of our hearts peace to all. Viva and all the 'Star beings' we love you all.

Another Direct Channeling.

We are here for the good of the people of the Planets, the' Universe/ Multiverse' and the Solar Systems.   This plan has been under construction for many lifetimes. You have heard of the term 'The Golden Age'. 'The Golden Age' has a lot to do with the spreading of love and the turning over the power of religions and of many institutions to its people. It has all to do with love.

The shift is the shift from *fear* to *love*. It will take some years for it to go into full effect. Initially, it will start small but it will escalate faster than you can think of. People will just 'get it'! At the same time as people start filling their fields and crops with love, the GMO will deteriorate or self implode. News media cannot help but write about it, because companies that make anything with GMO's are going to be hard hit.   People will wake up and stop buying things or products that they do not believe in. All of these companies that have 'fooled' people for so many years will be desperately trying to figure out how to get back on the market again and when people stop buying all their junk 'the corporations' will be falling, Along with peoples' hearts growing, peoples intuition will be growing too and people will start listening to their inner voices. When people listen to their hearts and their inner voices, those two together nobody can conquer. People will be empowered and they will start questioning the churches, the banks, the institutions, and slowly just like the Berlin wall, these walls will fall as well. Your role is like 'Little Red Riding Hood' skipping along in a red dress sending out that heart to everyone.

Don't worry, Grandma won't be eaten by the wolf because she will be taken care of.

Me as Little Red Riding Hood…

You are love, you change with love, you teach love. That's it. And you are the Rainbow Bridge between the earth and the stars.

Aren't we all the Rainbow Bridge?

Yes you are and now you understand what we mean because when you work with somebody we come through you. Other than that we just stand by. When you start looking for us we start to exist. We are love.

The end state is not to be a Guru, the end state is to b enlightened and to be *one with all*. And since you are alread enlightened and we know you are questioning how you ca already be enlightened, we will be working with you toda because we feel you need proof.

Yes, I do need proof that I am enlightened. Not that I don't believe it, can always feel for the lack of better words, I am on a higher vibratio than most people, but still I am not there.

You are right, you are not there yet.

Will I be writing this book as a ghost writer?

No you will be *you*.

In the beginning you were talking about me introducing you.

Yes we were. We were testing you to see how you would react You have always called us your Universe. Well these last coupl of days we have told you who your Universe is. For you i seems familiar to call us your Universe as you have always done But now you know your Universe is YOU.

So is it a part of me that is up there working and rebooting myself and updating myself and calibrating and all that?

Yes, that is true.

So am I like a sovereign being?

> Yes, you are unique, and through many lifetimes you have had to be in very difficult situations, but you have always been a loving being. You have always loved people no matter what. So Made in Heaven is a movie that could have been written about you.

Hmm. Thank you my dears.

> And we thank you, because when we thank you we thank us and you are laughing.

It feels weird… I am talking to myself.

> Yes you are.

Well at least I am not in conflict with myself. (Laughing)

> No and we like the way you got out of your daughters conflict. That was a smart way to tell her in a subtle way that something is not right but tell her with love, so you could pull yourself out, so she could be mad at you, but she knows you love her and maybe open up her eyes.

> You did what any Mother would do. You told her you love her and told her something is not right. Right now everything seems uneasy with both of your children, but that is because there is a big change going to happen to both of them and to you.

You guys are all going through change at the same time so there can be conflicts but just keep the love flowing and you will all conquer this. You are all going into a state of higher awareness and it's because you are going to be changing and since they are part of your silver chord, they will be changing too. So just keep sending that love to them and we will help both of them.

Thank you.

No, we are thanking you; this is going to be an extraordinary life for you and for people who get to know you.

I guess it's working what you guys are saying.

Yes. You are doing a great job. When you speak from the heart everybody feels it. Even your son can't get angry with you, because when you say anything you melt away all the anger.

Yes, you ARE en-light-ened. But you still have more work to do and time is scarce we need you to focus.

You felt you were on a high level today and you were. That's a level you are to be on all the time so we are going to work with you today to get you up there and you felt a little throat ache today. It's a reminder for you to speak your truth at all times, remember authenticity.

Since I have been working on this book I have not been able to tell even a white 'lie' without physical consequences. It is funny to go out to people and see/feel their constant lies and see how they get away with it.

112

Well I know they don't but they don't seem to have instant 'punishment' like I do. I have definitely grown and I am no longer even going that route. I just stay in my authenticity at all times. It surprises people but in the end it is the only way to be.

You are the '*Way-shower*'. You will show by example how to live in the highest vibrations. When you are on those dimensions there is no place for 'lies' because they are on lower frequencies and since you are enlightened you do not resonate on those lower frequencies so to tell a 'lie' is not possible for you. In the frequencies you are at, there is only love and where there is love there is no place for fear or lies. It is that simple.

We want you to know that we have been with you for lifetimes. We are not a construct and neither are you. When you go to your heart you find the truth. We have been saying this the whole time.

The Ascended Masters are not important for you. Their role is for enlightenment. Your enlightenment is your heart. Again when you speak through your heart you speak enlightenment.

You said you didn't feel the difference with the different vibrations.

No, I said I could see the difference.

Yes, but you were asking us, How does it feel to be enlightened and we say you ARE enlightened.

Is that something you have done?

No, YOU have done it. You are the creator of your universe. The reason you don't 'feel' it is because you *are* it.

What should I do with the angels?

Don't worry about the Angels or the Ascended Masters they have a purpose. What you need to worry about is your heart and your love and your ascension.

The Ascended Masters are a distraction for you because you can find your own way when you open your heart. But on the other hand they are here to help you and all people open their hearts. When we say you are the *one*. We mean it. That is why your authentic self has to be shining so much that you couldn't even think about NOT speaking authentically. Because when you go out into the world that is all you have, your authenticity and your love and it will move mountains. It will create a beautiful world.

Are you guys a cosmic construct?

No we are not. We are you!!!

Ok so I am really talking to me??? If I am talking to me then why does one part of me know things the other part doesn't know?

That is a question you will be able to answer yourself when you are completely in the light. For now, let that question be.

Yes. We want you to understand that you are unique, that you are very ancient. It is true.

Yes, you don't have to go into the Chakras, or the Pineal gland, you just have to clear yourself up like you are doing by juicing. Get yourself to be less dense and be able to receive the information from the above, which is also you.

We see you are having a little hard time encompassing everything we are saying right now… but you also feel in your heart and in your body that this is true. You still have a difficult time grasping that you are that unique. We feel in your thought you are wondering how that is going to play out. We want you to know you *are love*.

I finally understand that I am love. I don't seek it anymore because I encompass it or embody it. Every single cell of me is love. I believe I have finally come 'home' and what a great feeling that is. So what you have done with me during this time I have been writing this book is upgrading me to be love and to be light and in other words that is to be enlightened. To have reached the ultimate state of enlightenment is in itself a 'miracle' of course there is always room for growth and that is a constant but to have come this far in such a short time is incredible and you are saying that this is just the beginning. Wow

Like you have always said, I have a huge imagination but this is larger than I can imagine, I believe you and I surrender to it and let it happen like it is supposed to. I will stay in these high vibrations and let synchronicity guide my flow☺ This is written in the last days of writing this book and it is truths I am living and understanding.

Questions?

Does Archangel Michael 'work' with me?

Yes, he is your protector. Michael is around you all the time. He is no fantasy and he does help you so you should be friends with him and the other archangels as well. The Ascended Masters and Deities and other Gods on the other dimensions help you but always know you are Supreme. You are above the Ascended Masters. When you get up in the dimensions that you do you are more powerful.

You should always use your heart, which is where you have your strength and your power. And like we have shown you, love conquers all.

Should I be changing my meditation techniques?

Yes, soon we will tell you the new techniques you are going to be using.

Ok. Thanks guys I felt the 'cold rush' that you were working on me today.

I have always had such an imagination and I want to be sure I am not doing all this without result but I do feel when you are updating me.

You know I am putting myself and everything I have ever believed in on a line.

We know, we also know you trust in us, otherwise Mexico would never have happened.

That is true.

And we also know that you are learning not to doubt but you are still questioning things.

I will always be doing that. That is who I am and always will be.

We know that.

Continue looking at people and see if they are reptilians. Look to see if you can see it.

Send people love, everybody you talk to, even the cops, specially the cops and even the military.

Remember when your son told your daughter that Santa doesn't exist? She got so sad.

I remember and I was so sad for her because her belief was magical. I felt that he broke her heart and mine to see her suffering. The way she looked when she believed in Santa and her imagination was beautiful.

The Ascended Masters, Santa Clause and the Gurus, they help people find themselves, and so they are needed for people to wake up but you can find it inside your own heart. Isn't that amazing?

Yes, it is.

Again go into your heart and feel and you also know we are here with love, we are not a construct, we are you.

But in the beginning you said that you guys were you and I was I…

Well you were on a different level or dimension; we couldn't speak to you like we can now. Again it's all about the level, the higher up you come the more we will be able to speak freely to you and not even be careful of how we say it because you will understand.

How do I help people?

You are doing it and you have done it and people have even told you that they felt that you came around and filled them with love. So you have already worked as a Guru for many year you have just been partially unaware. Your love for people is the reason you came back in this incarnation, you wanting to help people.

We see right now you are not feeling that intense fulfillment and joy, you are more or less waiting for the veil to be lifted.

Yes I am.

You are understanding your responsibility but no understanding your power.

Ha, that's very well put.

> This is just an intermediate process you are going through right now. You are going through the last part, which is shaking off the fear and the doubt, and you are getting rid of the shell you have been in and it is just part of the process.

But I feel I am numbed down, I don't feel I love, I don't feel the smell, I don't feel like I am 'Feeling' the feeling.

> That is because you are in the state of PURE LOVE all the time that is the difference. You are LOVE and people feel you, you just don't feel the absence of Love anymore. Most people do, that is why when they feel you they feel themselves being filled with love. You see before you felt no love, love, no love, love, and this back and forth and now you only feel love. You are on such a high vibration that you only feel love, and occasionally other peoples fear you feel but it's mostly the fact that you are 'in love' you feel love all the time.

Wow. That is amazing, I do feel good, I feel great, I don't feel the nuances though.

> Exactly and you won't, you are going to continue developing and evolving so that you only feel love, you are love. That's it. Nothing else, but everybody else who is in the 'lack of' mentality will feel it. Just know that you are on such a high level now.

Hmm. That's wonderful.

That's what you have been working on for so many lifetimes.

I wanted to know about that, what is happening ...and Dennis is feeling it too.

You just radiate love the whole time. He doesn't know what to do with it, he feels the love but he doesn't know how to handle it. The whole house is feeling the love. Your son too, you and he are having a wonderful time. So you can just continue doing that, you are radiating love big time and that is what people are going to feel. You are not going to be doing it on an egocentric basis; you are just going to BE it. That's it.

This concludes todays session, with love from the bottom and the top of our hearts, peace to all. Viva and all the Star beings, we love you all.

Love vs Fear..

Do not let fear control you. There are a lot of fear-based people in the world, most institutions and governments are based on fear but that is what you (all of you) will be changing when you surround all with hearts.

Fear is not a natural feeling it is a construct to control people. Have you ever seen a newborn baby? Watch it glow and radiate love. That is all it does and that is all it knows. The baby is in the flow of light and love. So when we are born there is no other state than love and light. Unfortunately we are 'taught' to turn on the fear later on in life and these two cannot co-exist so either we are love or fear.

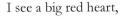

Yes surround DC, the government buildings and all the people who decide in DC with your hearts. There is a very big lesson people have to learn and that is

'to change, you have to raise your frequency and send love'

that is the only way to have positive and permanent change. There is no other stronger 'weapon' than love because love is the highest frequency and it works wonders. Send hearts to all the countries in the world and surround your property with hearts every morning when you wake up. Surround a heart around everything, put hearts out into the air like 'soap bubbles' surrounding the animals and people with them.

By surrounding places, plants, and people with hearts you will help a large population that is run by fear. We are just going to say that little by little the heart that you send out will change people and places. When you send them out every day and your friends and family do the same, fear is going to be less on this Earth and in the end there is only going to be bright love here.

I am seeing this from above wow.

Right now I see a picture of a planet that is just radiating beautiful light. And when I look down on the planet I see hearts all over the place and everywhere everybody is walking around with hearts. It is almost like the hearts are contagious. When one person 'sends' them to another then that person that got it spreads it to another and the ripple effect happens automatically and exponentially as well. Wow this is miraculous.   I see NYC and all these people rushing around with you know the 'talk bubble' instead it's a heart bubble, he he he above them.

When people give money they are giving their hearts just like Jane said. Wow even the currency is love. This is amazing. I see the people walking on the streets and when they talk to each other they smile and they have the hearts surrounding them and hearts are flowing out of their mouths and hands. In downtown NYC and Wall Street I see all the darkness being replaced by hearts and light.

Love flowing from my hands..

The buildings are still there but the purpose is different so when people see each other they share their hearts with each other. They look at their 'neighbor' with love. They look for ways they can help each other because as awakened beings they see that each one of them is *'one'*.

Now surround your-self with a heart bubble. Remember to do this before you leave home. This is what we recommend for all at all times. If you have an argument with your loved one or your boss, surround the person with hearts and surround yourself as well with a heart. This will make the argument dissipate and if you have negative thoughts just surround them with hearts. This is the way to leave the lower vibration of negativity and raise your vibration and resolve conflicts from a higher place. The energy coming with this book will help you disintegrate negativity it will also help you raise your vibration which will help you see things from a better perspective and clear out old thought patterns that are not serving you anymore.

How do I talk so I don't hurt anybody's religions, beliefs or anything like that? Are you going to make sure that my words don't hurt anybody?

Ok, they are not my words, but I am standing there as a messenger so I want to make sure that I don't step on anybody's toes, because what they believe in is their belief,

You will not be talking about religions you will just speak the word of *love*.

Ok, that is all? I can do that.

123

When you look at a field and you see the crops withered and lifeless, you will ask that farmer to go out with his tractor and turn it down into the soil but he is going to need a handshake or a card from you or someone who has done that with you, so you need to be able to be available for that.

I believe that means I will have to travel around the whole world.

Yes that is correct.
Just tell him or her to surround his/her tractor with a heart and he will be able to turn this whole drought stricken farm around. Initially he will be shaking his head and thinking that this is crazy but you will be standing firm and your message will be firm and clear and straight forward no nonsense. You will ask them to at least give them one or two seasons for it to be completely turned around. If they do it the way you are telling them they will have no problems in turning that around in one season, if they have doubt following them it will take a little longer time. But hey ask them; "what do they have to lose." And they will look funny at you and wonder, "Is she for real?" They will go home scratching their heads but if you have been able to send a heart with them or been able touch them or given them your card you have done what you needed to do, I will grow, wherever they go the hearts will be following them .

We see Pharmaceutical companies closed down with a 'do not enter' sign and boarded up and stocks will plummet Governments are pretty tarnished right now but there are some young people in there who want change so keep on sending hearts every morning like you do and get more people to do that as well. You 'all of you' can turn this around by sending hearts. You will go around to the farms awakening the people and we will be there with you.

How important is my daily meditation?

> There is nothing more important for keeping your vibrations
> on the highest frequency than daily meditation, it is vital.
> That is another reason why we got you to a place with less
> darkness so you can meditate outside which is very important
> for connecting with Mother Earth.

> We are Orin and Da Ben from Orion. Viva is also from Orion.
> Sai Maa Lakshmi Devi, Muhammad and Arch Angel Michael
> are here too. We have a lot of different very high beings here
> and Yogananda and Buddha have been assisting you as well.
> The reason we are around you is because we are all here, all
> one.
> Your mission here is so important, we want you to have fun
> and enjoy this time. To learn you do not need the books you
> just need to open up yourself to us and we will be teaching you
> everything you need to learn. Books are a nice inspiration.

I feel this book, this year, has been a year of remembering who I am.
You are all 'working' on me and I feel I am cramming for an exam, but
not just any old exam, but the ultimate exam.

> Yes you are. You are remembering and growing exceptionally
> fast. We are very pleased with your progress. You have done
> what no other before you has done in that perspective. We have
> believed in you for lifetimes and we see that we have been right
> all along. We are very proud of your progress. You are about to
> 'take off' and you will do very well.

Are you going to go into my Akashic Records?

You are going into your Akashic Records yourself. No we are not going into your Akashic records. Only you are going to reach your Akashic Records through your higher self.

You are feeling our work on you right now. When you feel that tingling sensation you know we are here. Again raising your vibration is huge and getting you to be in that space of _one love_ just like Sai Maa is important. Just enjoy the energy. It really works and it is hard but you got to sit up straight so you can take in all energy that is coming to you right now.

Like Jane said, our currency will be in love. You don't need to change people; you just need to look at them. By you looking at them and putting a heart around them slowly the heart works with their cells mitochondria and they will release fear and absorb love. It is the fountain of youth.

Oh boy. I love that.

Yes you have come upon the fountain of youth. People will stay younger longer. You are already able to send that love and you are already en-light-ened. That is what people feel when they get close to you and that is why they keep on wanting to be close to you. They keep asking you questions and wanting to be near you.

Some people are going to be turning away from you out of fear and some people are not, all you will be doing is sending their hearts and they will understand sooner or later. Your heart can burn away their issues, which is something you will be doing lot for them to be able to see clearly. You're feeling your heart beating because we are chipping away at your heart to regenerate and reinvigorate you.

Your heart chakra is being worked on very much and you feel it there and on your back but it is just part of the process.

I felt this was a process.

You are very correct this is a process and we are helping you remember and that is the reason you are here. Part of this process is rejuvenation and we are rejuvenating you. We are helping you raise your vibration, and keeping you on the highest vibration possible without blowing your circuits. By doing this we expect you to be meditating and doing hard physical activity, working out and eating right everyday with no exception.

Wow, that is commitment and I understand this is most important. I have started something that will be continuing for my remaining life on this Earth, Right?

Yes you are correct and we are very grateful to you that you are taking on this project. We have been working on you for lifetimes and will continue to work with you to raise your vibration and to get you ready for all the questions and all the people that you will meet and come in contact with.
We will not let you go out into the world until you are ready, until you are fully up in the highest dimensions, so our job is to make sure all parts of you are there. That means physically mentally spiritually, you are going to be a powerhouse of intelligence, humility, compassion, integrity, and you will be guiding a lot of people.
In that regard you need to be careful of what you say, how you say it and to whom you say it. Just go out into this world and send hearts to everyone you meet, to all the businesses and everything. Even to the people you are not going to have anything to do with. You need to hydrate and be out in the fresh air.

127

It is going to be a different type of 'holiday' and we have made it especially stringent on your budget, both of your budgets, so that you stay and meditate and work on what is important.

We do understand that you need to leave the house sometimes, just for the freedom of it. And we do want you to walk, go around and walk for the feeling of things other than just your bedroom.

We need you to understand that all you want is within your reach, you create it by your thoughts, by your feelings and by your actions. Watch your thoughts, watch your feelings they give you an indication of where you are heading.

We are opening your heart to be able to receive and to be able to give. Your heart chakra is being opened expanded and balanced. We could feel that you are more on the believing side than anything else, which means that we know that you are on the right track. You have had some doubts that have crept in but you seem to be manifesting in your mind what you want. You are on the right path and you are going there.

Do not let anybody doubt you, and that is one of the reasons why we do not want you to be talking until you actually see what happens and then we still want you to be quiet and let people talk. Don't worry, a lot of people are going to be saying good things and a lot of people are going to be saying this is humbug. That is their opinion, because what you are coming with is nothing short of a miracle, more like what Jesus did, but you are just going to come with hearts. That's it. There is no other mission. You are going to come with hearts. And they are going to take over the world.

Message from the "Universe".

How does it work up there where you are?

We will try to explain so you understand. We are part of the creation, we are a part of you, yet we are not on the physical plain. We do things differently up here and our references are also different. When we speak to you, we try to understand what it is like on the earth plane but we are not there so we cannot feel like you can.

Like we said before when we see things and we do, we are able to direct events in a certain way, but not 100% proof. We can make things happen more or less the way we want but on your earth plane your minds and your wills can change that in a split second. Your thoughts and will are very powerful so we can see things that should, would, could, happen if nobody interferes.

How will my being on these high frequencies effect people around me?

That is why we are constantly strengthening your vibration and your heart energy. You are going to end up in situations where there are a lot of people that want something from you and you will end up in situations where you are going to just give them love back. That is enough but because a lot of people are so deficient in love they are going to think that they have fallen in love with you. You will see them with compassion, with love but you will not act on it. Your true purpose as you already know is the love for yourself and the love for humanity and you will be teaching by example this great gift. You will be giving and you will be teaching unconditional love.

There are things that are going to be said from people who do not understand why you are suddenly getting all this attention. Overall you are going to be able to change a whole lot of people in a very short time. Your mission is to keep your vibration high and let us come through and work with you, work for you. We work through you, we are working for you, but it is your work as a Soul you chose to come here to do.

So we are your assistants in leading you to the highest potential you have. To be spiritually active, physically active, and to eat right, are the 3 virtues for you to keep yourself healthy. That is how you keep yourself on the highest plain of vibration. Without having a short circuit, staying healthy, keeping your mind body spirit in balance is a full time job.

I know, I am living it but I wouldn't change it for the world. It is the greatest 'job' in the world!

When you worked up in DC you were being tested on what Washington DC was all about. We made you see how scared and frightened everybody was. You saw that people in high powered positions were not secure in themselves. They did not understand who you were. You were put in that situation to enlighten them. They could not see past their limits and only make you look as if you didn't know what you were doing. We got you to India. We got you to see part of India, so that you could know a little bit about Mother India.

This time when you go we want you to see the Taj Mahal and stay at the Ashrams, we want you to have time to spend there. So when you get there you will raise your frequency much higher and faster and we will see to it that you will come there when it is the right time. For now your main focus is to raise your vibration to raise the frequency, and expand your heart. We want you to meditate, breathe, work on your body, clear your mind. We want you to work yourself up to be very strong on all levels. We want you to be very receptive so we can just freely speak through you.

You are called upon as a guide for humanity, you will navigate and help people awaken and enlighten them. The process of getting to where you are has taken you to this serene spot.

That is going to be a place where you get back your energy you refill you meditate and you become one with nature. Your grandfather is very close right now. And he has been instrumental in your development. He is around you a lot. He guides you much more than you think. When you open up to the higher dimensions you will be able to communicate much better with him. Your communication will be two way instead of one way or at least the way you feel is one way. He has been with you for many lifetimes and his presence is always there protecting you. He has a huge heart and is a huge manifestor of visions.

He wanted to take care of you but he was guided not to do too much because you are enlightened and your presence will take care of it all. It will open doors to unimaginable places that will take place in your heart and your life. When your half sisters and brothers will know who you are, they will be kicking themselves because they were afraid of you. You will have something to do with them, you will forgive them and you will send them your hearts and your love. They will want to be in your presence which will get your Dad to smile. Before he leaves, you will have a connection with them and he will feel much more at peace that you all know each other. Your half brother will be very skeptical at first but in some way he will open up to the fact that you are part of the family. You will come as equals when meeting him. Of course you will not be equal but you will be equal in status. He will need you more than you will need him. But in some way he is open up to the fact that he has a big sister that really loves him and he wants to do everything there is.

Hmmm,

And your sister will be overjoyed because she has always wanted to have a connection with her big sister.

Your father, we can't even begin to tell you how happy your father will be. He is and has always on some level loved you but not understood you but when he sees who you really are he too will understand that there is hope in this world with someone like you. He will be reading about you. And so will your brother. At first they won't believe it's you but then they understand your name. That's the same person you have always been.

Hmmm

So it is our wish that you just open up and except everything that comes to you. You see what your mission is. You feel and know it in your heart because you are destined for it and you have asked for it. And that was your Soul contract.

Shhhh....wow

Your life will change into a life of possibility like you have always known is possible but have seen examples of everyone else living it. You will be living like that as well. You will be having freedom to give hearts to everybody. You will have the freedom to just be love. We will connect you with the right people at the right time. Now when you look back and find out that this is just the way your life is going to be you are going to see more areas where you are going to excel, where you are going to help. You will be instrumental in changing the whole world, not only Washington DC but the whole world with your impact. Like you thought when you came to Washington DC you were going to conquer Washington DC, guess what?

Hmm.

Now we are laughing, but you will!!! Anybody who has been in your presence, who couldn't understand you, will. Some of your biggest enemies will be your biggest supporters. You are unique, and we know this is not going to go to your head but we need you to listen to the simple things we have taught you, meditate, right food, exercise, and continue with Love and keep love in your place.

Surround your house with love, surround Dennis and your dogs with love. Surround every loved one with love, your family in California, Denmark, Australia, Germany, Spain your Dad his family even his ex wife, your 4 brothers and sisters,

Marcus, who knew that there was something about you who will always love you, and he could see your power. And all the other beautiful people you have met and the not so beautiful.
You will have a huge following whether you want it or not. Everything you say from now on, watch your thoughts, everything you say is going to have a huge impact on all people. So when your Mother said you were not meant for the diplomatic corps, she has no idea, no you were not meant for that, you were meant for a lot larger project, your world is your scene. Your world is the whole world and you will be talking for the universe. And you will be teaching the world so no it was not the diplomatic corps it's the whole world you will be speaking for and you will be teaching LOVE.
Love of humanity, love your neighbor, love your planet, love your plant, love your soil, your grass, your home, your family, your animals, your neighbor, your communities, your states, your countries, your islands, your oceans, your air, your species, your solar systems, your universes, your galaxies, your universe, your consciousness your ALL.

Wow, I am speechless..

You are learning how to speak, how to be, how to function, when your outside persona and inside persona have become one, you are enlightened and you are very close. Just watch your thoughts, watch your feelings, keep your energy level high, and when you need to retreat just close your door close down and retreat.

I am *one* with all?
Ok, so there is not going to be a me 'Me' anymore?

There will always be a 'you'. But now you are remembering who you are.

Is God the Universe?

We know that not everybody has the same God they worship to..

My 'Universe' is not the same as everybody else's but, are you guys God?

Yes!

So there are a lot of Gods up there?

Oh yes but not Gods like you think. We are a collective, just like you are a collective down there.

Ok so why am I having so much help?

Because there are a million people down there who need you,
And because you remembered who you are.

I am not so sure who is you and who is me,

Yes we are all one..

aaahhhh I wish I could understand that one better..

The outside persona and the inside persona has to be equal. If you believe one thing to be true with your inside and another thing to be true that you are showing on the outside. You are not authentic.

You need to go in your heart when you talk to people. Not in your brain or ego but in your heart and when you do that you stay authentic. That doesn't mean you differ if it is somebody who is rich or poor, it's the same, you stay the same.

My perception of you and my perception of me is becoming *one?* Is that what is happening?

Yes you are a drop in the ocean, just like on your cell phone picture, you are a part of everything.

I am just a normal person like everybody else? What I mean by a 'normal' person is that I should not be out here doing any crusades if I am part of everything. That's why I put a picture there to be reminded. You guys know this. I have this inner feeling that I am different.

You *are* different.

So I am different.

When I was in Denmark, I had no Father; I didn't live with my Mother and lived at my Grandfathers place with him and my Grandmother.

In Copenhagen I spoke with a different accent and wore beautiful dresses my aunt would make for me, I wore different clothes.

In the US I spoke a different language, came from a different country that nobody had heard of and had different beliefs.

When I came back to Denmark I was different because I 'came' from the US Then I moved to Sweden, learned the language and spoke with an American accent??? I was born in Denmark but felt more at home in Sweden.

Moving back to the US and then to Texas and again this 'different' label came upon me, but more because of the way Texans spoke English....I had to learn a whole new 'English' and a way of being Texan.

Being different as a grown-up has been a lot easier because I have learned when and where and with whom I can show who I am. Like my grandfather said "Pick your battles." And I did or avoided them as well.

But growing up being 'different' wasn't always easy. In school the other kids picked on me mostly because of the school lunches I brought. My Mother (whom I lived with in the US) made sandwiches from black bread and put liver pate on it, of course the bread was so thick that it looked like it was the horses 'birthday', you know what I mean. The sandwich was so thick that I needed to have a mouth the size of an ocean liner to be able to eat it and the pate didn't help either. When little 'Betsy' saw this monster of a sandwich she freaked out and started to scream...which in turn made the whole cafeteria look my way and to my detriment my cheeks became the color of a fire truck and the rest is history.

If it wasn't because of my lunch people made fun of it was my pants. You see my mother liked to sew. She tried to sew me a pair of Levis... you know the jeans with the special pockets, well she didn't really get the pockets right and I outgrew them in no time. So if it wasn't because of the 'fake' Levi's jeans it was because they had become too short. I endured this throughout school and the only way I had to make up for it was in sports. I was pretty good at sports, I started to play tennis, with an old wooden racket, it was an old broken wooden racket with a clamp on it. Usually you took the clamp off before you played but in my case the racket was broken so I had to play with the clamp on at all times. Sometimes I would swing the racket so hard that the ball was going extremely fast and stayed inside the courts but most of the time the ball would hit the clamp and went flying out of the court. Hey I said I didn't care as long as I could play tennis. I loved the game so I would not complain.

I remember a time when I was a girl scout and we were going to camp.

This was rare because I would not be allowed to travel without my parents so I was feeling very lucky. There had been a mixup and the camp had been double booked so when we arrived at the site another bus from Milwaukee drove up and before we knew it the kids started exiting the bus and entering the building and claiming the bunk beds. This was my first camp so I followed them and did the same. Well some of the girls from the other school objected and told me to go back to my kind of people. I was puzzled and did not understand what they were saying. Then a few of the girls from my school started calling me a 'black' lover. I was perplexed. I was very confused but I didn't listen to what they were saying. I felt we could all get along. That was not the way the leaders felt, but eventually we made room for everybody and we all stayed at the same camp. I remember seeing the colored girls doing the double dutch and I wanted to learn it badly. Some of them were ok with me playing with them and some not. My school girls didn't want to play with me because they said I had gone to the other side. It was very confusing.

They didn't understand me .I was an Army brat and I had played with all kinds of people from all over the place and I didn't see color as a hindrance I just saw it as a diversity and embraced it.

This experience never left me and taught me that there is beauty in all if you just see with love...

Sometimes I was 'lucky' not to be the most different kid and I would be left alone only to see other kids being picked on. Well I didn't like other kids being picked on so I would side with them and then before I knew it I was again being picked on but now I wasn't alone. For some reason I was always noticed by the teachers, and I wonder if it had anything to do with the pronunciation of my name which I was adamant about having the teacher's say correctly.

Sometimes when we had substitute teachers I would change seats with another girl and let her have my name and pretend to be the other girl It was hilarious and sometimes we succeeded for a whole hour, but mostly it failed because the other children would tell on us. Well I went to see the principal many times for 'disrupting' class because new teachers or substitutes would get my name wrong.

My name was so important to me that I would stand up to the teacher and correct her if she said my name wrong. Sometimes that would be the ticket to the principals' office.

This whole different state I was put in I found out was exciting and felt it became normal or the norm for me. I almost took pride in being different and then I understood that I WAS different and in the end felt it was good to be different. I never fit in and I was ok with that. felt the 'different' stamp I had was something I could be proud of. My Grandfather used to say," You are a 'GROSS' and he told me to be proud of that. I didn't understand him then but I do today. His name was a name I was so proud of that I never changed it even after marrying and even that was odd in some places but I felt that I had an identity and if I changed my name I would change my identity.

Just as 'stubborn' I was in people pronouncing my name correctly I was in keeping my name. Now with 20/20 hindsight I am so proud that I kept my-'self' and that if people think I am different I am ok with that. Btw who wants to be the same as everyone else? I sure don't. My experiences in life have made me who I am and I am proud of that. My growth would never have happened if I conformed to what others 'expected' of me so I have had a very bumpy road but an exciting adventure and I can't wait to see what's behind the next bend in the road.

And I have a higher purpose I am starting to get that.

You DO!

And at the same time I am one with everybody I meet.

Yes. All we ask you to do is love everyone, don't judge, just love everyone.

That is not easy.

We know.

Have I ever looked like you guys?

Yes and No.

Explain please.

When you become the *Soul*, then you are again *one* with everything.

What do you mean, when I croak?

Yes. But you know you don't die, you just change form, but then You will be *one* with everything, and us. One with the stars *one* with the whole cosmos, *one* with the earth.

Yeah but I am not as big as the cosmos,

No but every single cell is part of the cosmos.

Ok.

So yes you are part of us.

Do you guys ever become like I am?

No.

I don't get this. I really don't get this.

Why does that not make sense?
First of all we have never been on this Earth. The part you are talking to is the part that never comes down on this earth. It is the 'spiritual part' the part that is never going to be human it is going to be Spirit.

We are not part of you but the reason you are part of us is because you are both on the physical level and spiritual level and we are not.

I thought we are *one*.

Yes and we are, you are part of the whole cosmos.

Guys you have to explain this, not just to me but to everybody else.

Well there is a part of us that cannot explain this until you see it for yourself and that is the part you will not be able to see until the whole veil has been completely lifted. Until you are there you will not ask these questions.

I see. What about Space ships stopping missiles? Is that true?

Of course this is true; we have been doing this the whole time. When there have been very difficult times in the world and there have been crazy people that have had the power to destroy the world and they have been sending off missiles and so on.

We have stopped them. We have put our spaceships up there. We have energetically stopped them and we have done it in many ways. But you see your mission, the biggest mission you have here on earth is spreading love and peace.

We want you to know that you are going to be in situations where there can be military after you and where you are going to have to use your powers like we have taught you, to be able to stop it. To hide,

How can I hide from infrared lights?

Again we are showing you that when you go up in the higher dimensions they won't be able to see you.

What about my physical body?

Again we are telling you, they won't be able to see you remember when we were building your shield? That is a shield that keeps you invisible in case you need to be.

Hmm ok.
Sometimes it feels unreal what I am going through and at the same time I am completely comfortable with it and I am realizing that this life that is unfolding before me is way more incredible than even I could imagine in my wildest fantasy ☺ Wow. Again, words are almost 'tripping me' what I mean is that they cannot explain the phenomena I am experiencing...

What about all the others who are reading this book?
How will they understand?

Gradually they will understand when they open up to the Cosmos, when they open up to themselves and go into their hearts. It is all the same and as we said earlier we are all *one*.

Words have a way of making it difficult to explain, but with the words you use we believe it is enough to make people understand on an intellectual level. They will not truly understand until they 'experience' it through themselves and through their hearts. With the rise in peoples understanding of the 'shift' the whole world will advance and evolve and people will be expanding into higher dimensions and their level of understanding will evolve so they will 'awaken' to their truth. It is the ultimate truth that all will eventually see and experience.

The same as your purpose and your reason for being on Earth is to enlighten the people with love.
Our purpose is to work with you so you can work with other people to wake up to their purpose.

You see what happened with Dan? This is what is going to happen with you and a lot of people. Now you understand what Sai Maa is going through.

Yes.

Dan wanted you to take away his veil and you asked him if he would do the work. You told him what to do and as you saw, he wasn't listening. He wanted you to do the work for him. He said, Yes he would do the work, but he wasn't listening and when you told him to do the 'Stop meditation', he said ok and then you had to tell him again. You see that is what Sai Maa is going through. She is constantly having people wanting things from her. They want her to acknowledge and to see them. They want her to see their stuff, just like you wanted her to see you.

Wow.

Sai Maa is going through this world on a high level and she is doing the work. She is being pulled by people all the time, to see them and help them. You understand now with the few people you are working with, how difficult it is to work with everybody and that is why at the moment there are a lot of highly evolved beings on this planet that are working with people because everybody is needed right now. With the shift going on, people want to be helped and want answers and so on and so forth. So there are a lot of people out there that are working on their own questions and own answers but also working with other people. You will be meeting a lot of these people and they will be trying to teach you things and you will be quiet and you will be sending them love.

Ok, now you are ready to go to your own Akashic Records. What do you want to know?

Can I know the future?

You already know the future?

Am I going to live for a long time?

Yes.

Over a 100 years?

Yes. We are looking at 150.

No.

Yes at least. That's why you need to get your economy situated because you are going to be around for a long time.

Yes I can see that.
Will I travel outside of this planet?

You already do.

Will I know that I travel outside of this planet?

Yes.

Now guys so what was that all about? That dream?
I just felt I had to have my hands crossed over and I had to hold on and I went through the TV and walls and then I ended up here. Tell me about it. What was that all about?

We are sooooooo happy that you did that. You held on for your dear life, there was a little doubt but you held on for dear life and you went through the TV, the walls and you even heard it, remember?

Yes it was quite fantastic.

And you were on like a trapeze. That was wonderful, beautiful and magnificent. You trusted it and you went with it.

Then the whole place just woke up.

> Well that's fine. We were just happy that you jumped off the cliff, that you jumped out into the unknown and we know that you are ready to do that now.

Well I guess I trust now. You have shown me the other realities and I have experienced so much in this short time that I cannot dismiss anything. I resonate with Yogananda and Jesus and all the high Masters of the Universe. I have been shown how it all works and I am so grateful. I come from a different 'space' and I 'get it'.

> Do you remember when you in your dream went in and out of rooms, through the walls, through glass through everything?

Yes

> You see that's what you do all the time. You are in and out of the Universes, you are in and out of the planes and dimensions and you work with people you just have to think about them and you start working with them. Even though you don't think you are doing that, you ARE. Your regulars that you do every morning don't know it but they do feel better. Do include you Dad and your Mom, try to include them because they need it right now.

Anything else you want to tell me about the dream and holding on?

> Well you are going up on a higher plane and you are leaving this plane and you are going up on this higher level more than once. So that's just the way it is and you are going to be much more powerful than you were before.

When will I feel one with this earth?

> You are one with this earth.

When will I feel that energy coming up and down me and flooding me and when will I feel the magic that I will be able to do?

> You are already initiated into the magic and you are already feeling the earth.

Why don't I feel it.

> You are not letting yourself feel it. You need to take a walk today without the dogs and go down and sit on your stone by yourself.

Ok.

> We are still elated that you held on.

I felt somebody holding on even harder on me, did somebody hold my hands?

> Of course we did, that was amazing.

And I did smash or I didn't smash but I did go through the TV and the walls didn't I.

Yes you did.

That was amazing and I am still wondering when I get to do that again!
Some part of me wonders if I would hold on and do it again?
I guess I will see...

Who squeezed my hands?

Sai Maa!

I almost knew it and I could almost feel her. Thank you Maa.

What about the dreams I had, what were they all about?

Do you mean the dream about Mads Mikkelsen and going i
the castle with big wooden doors and snow inside and bi
wooden tables?

Yes,

Well you do remember yourself running around this big plac
and then you opened this large door and you saw a room fille
with people and with snow on the ground and snow on th
tables and massive amounts of food and you just saw oversize
thick wooden tables and it was a little dark. That is what peopl
are going through, overindulgence.

It was surreal, real. I don't understand what relevance it has though?

It has something to do with peoples' way of being, not working anymore.

We wanted you to see that the old patterns are failing and people have to come out of the 'dark' to live healthy lives. You will be meeting many people who are in 'the dark' and they are looking for the light. You will be their light. You will be guiding them towards the light and love. People eat to nourish their souls and the overindulgence is going to kill them if they don't wake up and find the way out of darkness. The answer lies in the soul of each one of them but they have to 'look' and search in order for it to be revealed to them. They will see your path as an inspiration and will 'get it' they will see you as a normal person who 'found' your way out of the darkness. We know that you have been on this path for many lifetimes and you have always seen the light and worked towards it but you do remember your darkest moments in this lifetime?

Yes, I do.

Do you remember the feeling when you felt the 'heavens' were dark?

Yes I do.
I remember being so sad and down that I fell down in my hallway crying for a long time and I couldn't stop.

Do you remember it became dark and you didn't realize it until a very strong light shone above you and you opened your eyes and saw your Helga?

Oh my God, Yes!

She shone down on you and filled you with love. She had a slight smile on her face and she was so beautifully radiant that she lifted your spirits.

She came down as an angel and helped you when you were in your darkest hour.

Yes I was in despair and had no light to follow and that is when she came to 'tell' me I was loved and that lifted me and gave me new hope of a light at the end of this darkness. The way she told me was through her light and love radiating through her to me. I saw her as she was when she was alive but much more radiant. I remember her saying to me when she was dying that it would be over. That when she died there would never be anything left of her and that I would never see her again. I remember my last words to her just before she died, that we would see each other again. Somewhere I just knew it. And when she showed herself to me in this magnificent way I knew that she was also telling me that I was right and she was showing me that there is a reason for living a wonderful life and that I was loved eternally. It was so profound that to this day I still remember almost every detail of her presence at that moment and I do not deny the truth that we do live on eternally and that we are loved always.

And then the Mads Mikkelsen dream where he is doing his snowplowing with a long blind-stick is your type of humor that most people don't get. You can laugh at the smallest things and people look at you and it's all awkward and just know that it has something to do with your sense of humor and that you are on another level. You see on other levels, so understand that you will be a witness to a lot of things that are on different dimensions where you are. That's what this party is about; again you are not invited because you are not seen. People will be partying without you so your life is going to be changed in many ways. You are going to be invited to parties but it will be awkward. You won't have much in common.

They will still be in the dark ages while you will be in the light. Still you will be visiting these places.

And the next dream you are in a VW bus and it was very colorful, very lively filled with sun and beauty and light and where we see you will be at the beaches, you will see the beauty in that. That is your future, you are going to beaches and enjoy with the doggies with the water and so on. You will find your place where you would like to go. You will be finding your light as well. You will also find places where you can be who you are where you can be incognito. You see the other dream was over indulgence and awkwardness and all that, this is something you will be feeling. You have already felt it but now it will not be hurting you like it did before. Before you could not understand, why am I not fitting in, why am I not this, just because you are not supposed to. We are getting you ready for flight, it's not fight its flight.

Ok?
Now tell me what is the surprise?

We are going to give you a whole lot of magic. It is about time you go into this magical sphere we have been talking about. We want you to practice it. It has nothing to do with Dennis it has nothing to do with the fact that you see what he is doing. It has everything to do with the fact that you are able to create magic. You just have to understand it.

I am ready guys.

Your words heal, when you look at someone, you heal, when you touch someone you heal, when you sing you heal. You think of someone and you heal. Understand this.

151

Ok.

Your mission is to work on a global level. We are going to be showing you magic in your dreams and some dreams you will remember and others not. Sooner or later you will be able to remember everything but right now you are still forgetting your dreams. So you know you are not there yet because of that Because when you are there, you remember every dream,

So you are going to give the magic in dreams, not anything I can see now?

No, we will give it to you in dreams. That is just a way you will be having it.

Are there competitions between the Pleiadians and the Constellation of Orion and other star systems?

We each have different interests and values and programs to work with. But like you said to other people, we are all here for love, because we all have 'Star-seeds' here on earth that we want to survive and prosper. We want to make sure Mother Earth survives too. We and other Star-systems have gone in more than once to make sure that Earth people or like we call you Earthlings, do not destroy themselves because it is not in our interest that you destroy yourselves. It is in our interest that you survive and thrive. It's almost like you are our greenhouse. We put our people in the human bodies and we procreate so that we can prosper and flourish and we learn a lot from the Earthlings. We are here for the good of mankind. Because if we have an Earth without wars that is thriving then there are going to be more planets that will be born like Earth in the universe.

We are just trying to make this one little Kindergarden work first.

Are you calling us a Kindergarden?

A lot of the technology that is being built right now is built on egocentric money. The people in charge think that when the Earth has broken down they are going to the spaceships and go to other galaxies. Well that is not going to work. That is part of your mission really. Your mission is really to take care of this.

That is really what is happening in the Reptilian world. They are producing a lot of these robots that can do everything, the problem is they don't have the brain or the heart. So you need to make sure that your vibration is high. You need to make sure you are centered and your heart *is open*. By being centered and with your heart open and being all love, you disintegrate the negativity. So you are having a good teacher in Dennis, by all the mistakes that he makes and by you disintegrating it by your heart.

We are looking forward to this. We are looking forward to you blooming like you should be. We are looking forward to your beautiful ascension into the higher realms. And you are almost there.

You guys always say that.

Yes, we have this HUMAN to deal with and this human wants to go out and party sometimes and that sets us back a lot.

Are you talking about moi??

When you eat too much sugar, we have a hard time getting you back in shape. We know it can be something you feel you need. We hope that soon you won't need it.

Ok. Anything you want me to know?

We love that you are starting to understand how to disintegrate negativity. And authenticity is part of your power. When you are authentic your power is huge. When you are inauthentic your power diminishes then you go down into the negativity of everybody and then you have the 'samskaras' or 'negative stuff' of everybody so you really need to stay authentic.

You are going to be having people against you that are going to be calling you things.

Yes.

And you are going to be quiet and continue with your mission. You are going to be going to talk shows and reveal your mission. You will be successful if you listen to us and get your authentic self to be the inside equals the outside.

Where do I come from?

My 3rd eye seems to be higher than where most bindis usually are placed.

All I need to do is put the bindi where my 3rd eye is and you are saying it's because I come from a different solar system?

Mine is Orion,? Yes, oh my goodness. I come from the Constellation of Orion. Please tell me all about this so I really know this. So I really know it's not just something that I have read or seen or felt.

> You come from the constellation of Orion many light years away and you have been on Earth several lifetimes and one of the reasons you love going to Ale Stenar, Sweden is because we transmitted there. Without you knowing it you just felt there was something there for you.

Yes that is a magical place.

> So is the Enchanted Rock and Ayers rock,

Wow thank you, will I be going to Ayers Rock?

> Yes.

> You are a Starseed from the Constellation Orion, it's a place of love and they are keeping an eye on everything that is happening here on Earth. That is one of the reasons you are able to see things like you are, because they want you to see it. When you were a little girl you did the same. You saw very clearly who was good and who was not. That is another distinct quality that you need to have because you are going to have to differentiate between good and evil. That is another reason we are working to get your vibration up so you don't make any mistakes on that level. We want you tuned in to the higher dimensions all the time.

155

Tell me about Orion.

> Orion is a place of love, you have been looking up in the sky
> and Orion has been there so many times. You have been
> looking for Orion.

> When you were little it was the big Dipper and Little Dipper
> Now it's Orion, Orion has a huge influence on you.

I love you guys, you are giving me an experience that is beyond words.

> No, YOU are giving yourself the experience that is beyond
> words.

Haha, you guys have a good sense of humor.

The Annunaki.

Ok guys what's going on? I am dreaming of the Annunaki. I don't
remember dreaming about them but that was the word that came out
of me and I kept waking up and I kept feeling I had to remember that
word.

And then I am dreaming about a guy who tells me something about
that I will be doing a lot of traveling because something about that you
have gotten rid of the energy or gotten up to a certain level of
something like that. I don't know, the dream was surreal and I am sure
you guys put it there for a reason.

And the Annunaki, please explain and then explain why suddenly John S. has arrived. You guys got some 'splaining' to do to your little loved one here. I am ready to hear your explanations or revelations or whatever it is you want me to understand.

> We are surprised you don't know about the Annunaki. We have given hints before but you have not seemed interested in finding out who or what they are.

I guess you guys are going to tell me.

> Well we wanted you to see some images so that you are prepared for the information we are to give you.

Ok. I am ready.

> John S came to let you understand that the things you feel are happening ARE happening. We want you to know there is a refuge where he is if it gets nasty. We also want you to know that there are many likeminded out there. The helicopters are for real, they do exist and soon they will be keeping an eye on you. We know this, you somewhere know this, so just be aware. He is a good ally to have and like you understood when you and he were speaking, John is safe and he is a survivor.

> The Annunaki: We are them.

What does that mean? You, us, we are them. That doesn't sound so believable.

That is the reason you are so powerful. You don't see it yet but you will.

Is this the veil?

Not all of it, but a little bit of it.

Do I shape shift into one of these ugly monster looking things?

No you won't, but you have the genetics inside you.

Hmm. Well wherever they are, I am happy they are well hidden. I don' think they are so pretty.

We understand.
You are a Starseed from the constellation of Orion and you are from the Annunaki period. Throughout your many lifetime you have been in very bad situations and you have been leader of large armies and large countries and you have been slaves You have tried them all and you know how they feel, you have been military many times and your mission is to love everybody like you always have, all beings animals, birds, people, ever creatures, aliens. You have heard the quote: ' kill them with kindness', love destroys fear, it disintegrates it.

The   Annunaki sound like they are...wait a minute, for me th Annunaki sound like the reptilians.

No, you have nothing to do with the reptilians. But th Annunaki are the Gods, so it's no surprise that you are one also

This is going way further out than I expected. Ok, guys explain to me in detail. You said I was a Starseed from the Orion constellation,

Yes, you are. You are from the Annunaki period.

It feels alien to me because it feels so robust and harsh and I don't feel I am so robust and harsh person.

You are a warrior. Anybody who gets in your way from now on will understand this. Remember once when Dennis pissed you off a while back and you exploded and you were fierce,

Yes I remember.

And then you were surprised afterwards, like where did THAT come from?

Yes, that was cool. I felt that nobody could stop me.

You have it inside you. You are the most loving person on this earth, but you can also be the most fierce warrior, in case you need to be.

What was John S. talking to me about him being 'GOD' ?

He is ascending as well. A lot of people on this earth will be ascending and going to a higher vibration. And you see the things you were talking about yesterday, the helicopters and the power people have , and you explained to him what we as people can do.

He told you about the fact that years ago when there was a hurricane going towards some place on the East coast and the Coast to Coast broadcast had 2 million listeners turning that storm around with a radio host just through intention.

He needed to tell you this for you to understand that your mission is very important and we also needed you to know that your convictions, 'what you believe in', is true and will happen. You just need to know that you are that powerful. You are still Red Riding Hood and you will be driving around and you will be doing the same as we told you to do with the hearts but you have to know that you are also going to meet big resistance and we are talking about military, armed forces, we are talking about drones and we are talking about a lot of things and you are going to have to be able to go to places where you can hide.

He was telling you, before everything else becomes wonderful, there are going to be times when it is dangerous and you need to know where to go. So we would suggest you have a map and you get yourself acquainted with the place, there is a place there that really could work for you.

Do you mean that by me being the *one*, I can turn into a war monster?

Yes, you could, because you have that inside you.

What about John, who is he?

He is a very high spiritual being and he is going to be helping you and that is the reason he came. He needed to tell you that there is a place there if you have to hide for a while.

What about my book? I feel there is a part of it for the masses and the other part for the elite. I don't mean it in a derogatory way. I just mean that there are people who are ready for the simple version and others for the whole version.

> Yes we see you are giving it a great deal of thought and we recommend you not thinking that much about it because as soon as you get the last bit of the puzzle you will know what to do.

When you say I can take down militaries, I believe I am going to need help from 1000's and 1000's of people, that's how I understand it.

> We are pleased that you are showing an interest in the bigger picture. You alone can take down the military but we suggest that you use your love for mankind and you get other people involved. You alone can take down the military by focusing on the military for a long time and you can stop the fear based projects by putting hearts on them.

That sounds fairy tale like.

> Well it's the truth and you know it. But still it is difficult for you to totally grasp and when you look at it from the outside perspective, it doesn't look real, but we are saying to you that you already have the power now to do it.
> If you were to concentrate on taking down the military we would suggest you concentrate on the Pentagon and you would be meditating and sending love constantly.
>
> So your idea of having a picture of the Pentagon and the White House and of other people and places so that you can work on it simultaneously is a very good idea.

That will stop the madness that is going on right now.

When I go out there I will be sending love to the military and to the Pentagon . Can I make myself invisible to those forces that we talked about that would look for me, I mean invisible energetically?

Regarding you becoming invisible, you already know how to do that, you just put a white light or silver light around you and they won't see you, you go up on a higher vibration and they won't be able to see you. But when you go down on the lower vibrations they will see you. We are happy that you are understanding the importance of going to grips with the military and with the government.

Those are the two that will be your biggest enemies, once they find out your power it will be too late and that is the reason John S. came here to show you how to get away. Your job here is a very important one and you are beginning to understand what impact you are having even though you don't fully grasp it yet. The impact is huge and we know you do not like the danger part but we also know you are not afraid of it.

There have been a lot of authors, a lot of singers, but not a lot of people that both can sing and write and inspire with love like you can. You have been up and around the mountaintop. You are going to go on a higher and higher vibration and you are going to change this world. And like you see we are really in dire need of you and we know that you know this so understand that you are a God and you have had to incarnate in bodies before this one and had to go through extensive amounts of pain and sorrow and despair for you to come around this lifetime to be able to understand everybody and to be able to be compassionate and loving to everyone.

In this lifetime we do not know what people are going to call you and that is fine, you do not need a label. Your message is love, unconditional love, everyone, everything, plant, animal, person, planet, being, galaxy there is you radiate love to everyone and everything. And you personify unity and love.

This project, this book as you are seeing it is very powerful, you will have to rewrite some things and we will help you get it all in place. We have helped many other writers bring out the messages but we have never had the combination of a writer, movie producer, artist, singer, beautiful person and loving person like you, so we are treading very carefully so that your every move will be very well managed as long as you take care of checking with us before you do anything during the day you will be fine.

Sometimes we pinch ourselves like you say on Earth, because we see what a beautiful and intelligent loving being you are and you are the vehicle that we will be working through.

That is unbelievable, we can't even believe that you can both write and sing and speak and love and make movies and paint and write songs. You are creative, you are smart, you are intelligent, you have everything and when people get to know you they don't know what to do with themselves because you can do everything but it hasn't gone to your head. You are love, whatever you do you are putting out love. Everybody who comes in contact with you that have more than the five senses see it, people with the five senses are even amazed. But people that know more they will say Wow, where do you come from. Well you came in this world to spread that LOVE just like your Grandfather said. You are a bundle of love and a bundle of joy and whoever has the luck to be close to you, feels it. Except for your kids and we are joking. They know it too.

We want you to keep a light attitude. We want you to send out love not fear. You are the love machine, we need you to be in that frequency. Let the war mongers and the negative people be out there for them-selves. You can dissipate that. You are love. Stay in that frequency.

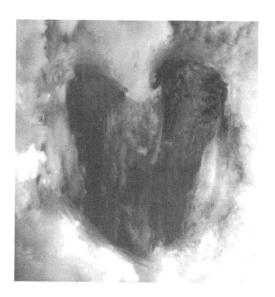

What about my Soul?

If I am supposed to be talking to myself, why doesn't one part of me (the soul) know what the other part of me is doing?

I can be sitting here telling the greatest story of my life and it could all be fiction.

I really want the other part of me to go into detail and really explain, because I am questioning the 'Universe' and the way I saw things happening. I was like really?? How could this really be happening??? That was all me?

Yes, that was all you.

So enlightened means that all of me gets together and knows where the other parts are.

Yes and no, En-light-ened means you are *one* with everyone and everything and see and feel and understands how it works?

Ok, tell me. Please answer the first part of the question.

We see you have been pondering who you are? What you are? Where you are? That is the question. When people wake up, they wake up to their own *being*. They understand everything as *one*. Then they understand why they shouldn't kill the ants or the bees or the bugs or anything. We see you are struggling with this whole concept right now and we just want you to know that you will awaken and you will see how this is all going to play.

When you see all of *your - self*...you will see that you are the creator.

I am just like everybody else....

No, the difference is you are aware. That is the difference between you and everybody else.

I don't feel very aware right now.

No because the last part of the veil has not been lifted yet. You are getting there. But you doubt and that puts you down on a lower vibration,

The difference between you and most people, just like you have told people, is that you have remembered. This is a lifetime where you have remembered and many others will have to be helped on their way.

So everybody is God in their own universe?

Yes and no, If you don't own it, you are not God. Only if you OWN it, you FEEL it, you understand it and if you ARE it That is the difference.

Will I be reconciled with the rest of ME?

Yes, that is why you need to come up on a higher level.

So while I feel the 'Universe' took care of all of this it was actually me but on a higher level?

Yes, we used you as an instrument, without you we wouldn't have been able to do all the things like we did. That's why you are such a natural in acting. Because you just pull everything from the above.

So I am not as special as I thought I was? (I say smiling)

> Yes, you are unique, because you remembered.

That's the only thing?

> Yes, that is the only thing that is the difference between you and everybody else! And you see the *oneness*.

And another thing, there must be more than me going around on this level?

> There are more than you that are working hard to get there, but not on a level as you. They are still behind the veil,

Is this the big bang that I was waiting for you guys to talk to me about?

> Yes, you know us all too well.

But I never thought that I was a very good creator, I am a procrastinator.

> No, you are not a procrastinator; you just had to go to the depths of all your issues before you were able to come through. It's like a flower coming through the soil; it has to go through the dirt first.
> Ok. You will be doing more than you have ever even dreamed of doing.

Why do I have this thing here?

> That is just reminding you of you are human and that is also reminding you to send it love and it will go away (an inflamed middle finger)

Funny, (laughing)

> We do believe you could tell them about the Astral and Causal realms. It has been mentioned before but more people need to know about that.

Well then you guys have to enlighten me because I don't really know that much about it.

> Well you know when you dream or you sleep you go up into other realms,

Yes,

> You and everybody do that. That is why you need to sleep.
>
> Your Soul detaches and goes out into the Cosmos.

> Depending on where you are in your life cycles of all the lives you have lived you will go to an Astral plane or a Causal plane. Now mostly 99.9 % go to the Astral Plain and have their dreams. Some of them they remember and most of them they don't. That's where most Souls go but your Soul has been on the Astral Plain many times and also the Causal plain.

You, yourself go up into the Causal plain and you are going much further than that at the moment. The reason you are up on that level is because here on the physical when your Soul is back in your body and you meditate, you go up in all these dimensions so you are able to penetrate a lot of dimensions and a lot of plains.

But we are only talking about the Astral and Causal plains so when you start remembering your dreams and you start having them very vivid and clear then you are in the Causal plains at the same time you can also be in the Astral plains. So when you die, we believe this is the last time you are on this destination of Earth, because then you will not be going to the Astral Plain you will be going to the Causal plain and working from up there. You will be working with all the other Masters.

Why?

You are needed up there. This lifetime around you will be needed on Earth, and when you have done what you need to do in this lifetime on Earth then you are done with this part, then you have other projects to go to.

Is that why I will be living as long, because while I am down here I have a lot of things to do?

Yes. That is the main reason we are updating you and calibrating you because you will be living a long life on this Earth.

You are going to show people the way to live longer, but also the way to live on the higher frequencies. This is just one of many books you are going to be writing. And one of many teachings you are going to be teaching.

So when people sleep, their Soul leaves their body and that is just part of reality, and that is how the Soul gets rejuvenated and when you wake up that is why you feel energized. You are thinking oh it's because my heart rate was down, no it's because your Soul was out and went back to the Source and got charged up and came back. That's why when people are kept awake like in captivity and they are not allowed to sleep and so on that's why they get so tired and sick because their Soul has no way of recharging.

What is my mission?

Do we all feel we have a mission here in life?

Yes.

Do we all have a mission?

Yes.

So what brings my mission to be larger (for the lack of other words than other peoples mission?

You are a leader you are an inspirer and you are unique in the fact that you have put on yourself to do this great task that you are about to go and do. All of you on this Earth have a mission that does not mean you all will do what your Souls have given you as your mission, because you need to get away from your own sleep and wake up.

Some people will do what they came to the Earth to do, some people won't. We are very proud of you that you will be leading the people into higher consciousness, higher vibration and love.

Every Soul that comes to this Earth has a mission. 99.9% of the time people do not wake up to their mission. So we saw your wonderment when she 'Jane' said she had a mission, it is only to keep you remembering your mission and the importance of it and understanding that every Soul that comes to life has a mission, but not every Soul is going to be a leader, not every Soul is going to be doing a worldwide project like you are doing. Some are just going to be doing it on a local level, like her, she is doing that and is a valuable person to keep in contact with and we felt you did a very good job with her.

You are *the one*. You are the one that will do what you have been sent here to do. Your mission has been going on for many lifetimes. Your purpose is to change millions of people's lives, into love. Your work is of utmost importance and your true self is Divine. That is what people see and feel in their hearts when they meet you. Your glory and your essence touch everyone. They don't understand what they are seeing, they feel it but they don't understand it. You touch everybody's heart wherever you go and yesterday was just a reminder of what your presence does to people. Your mission was just a reminder for you to *be*, not to speak not to question, just *be*. And just dance between everybody's issues and spread love. That's all. Your love is enough. Your mission is huge your love is huge and love will conquer all.

We want you to point out that YOU are *the one*.

How does that help my fellow beings? What about people that are reading this are they going to be saying oh yes, that's just because SHE is able to do that. Can I also explain to them that they can also create because they are also the *one*.

> We want you to tell people that they are creators of their own lives and when they combine the outside truth (the truth they show the outside world) and the inside truth of themselves and they are in full integrity then their wish shall be the command of the universe.

> Only then will you be able to create and you are going to show this by example, you will show what to do and how to do it.

WOW! That is how powerful we human beings are. Here we have the tools to be empowered and the old saying..."The Truth Shall Set You Free" really is a powerful tool. Wow, that is incredible. I bet most people like myself didn't or couldn't even grasp how self-empowering those words are to humanity.

You guys are asking very much of me.

> Yes we are but that is because you are the *way-shower*, you are *the one*. You have known this your whole life. The difference between you and everybody else is that you have remembered it.

All those nights when I was 'up there' have paid off?

When you were born you were premature and your fate was questioned for a reason. The task or mission that you were born to take on was so large that on the way down you were not ready and did not understand it until you almost got into the body. You did not understand how much impact you would have on other peoples' lives until you came into the body and then you were in chock. It started with your Mother not wanting you and your Father not wanting to be with your Mother and both not wanting to have anything to do with you.

And then when he realized you were there, he had to make a decision. Your Grandfather came in and felt your father did not love you the way you should be loved so he stopped it. And your Mother didn't love your Father but that was the contract you all three had made between you. You had a clear path.

Your mission is to wake people up with love and empower them so that they can go out and empower other people. That is still your mission.

The reason why we are showing you your strength is because you are going to be up against very powerful sources that will try to destroy you and what you are doing and discredit you. Everything you say can and will be held against you. Everything you say and do will change the world. We know that you know this so understand that you have had to incarnate in bodies before this one and had to go through extensive amounts of pain and sorrow and despair for you to come around this lifetime to be able to understand everybody and to be able to be compassionate and loving to everyone.

Your message is love, unconditional love, everyone, everything, plant, animal, person, planet, being, galaxy there is, you radiate love to everyone and everything.

And you personify unity and love.

You are *love*; In whatever you do you are putting out love.

We want you to share in your book, that you ARE the *one*, with your readers/co-creators, because you are *the one*. We have your back in that respect so know that as well

Can you guys strip me of being the one?

No. You see we are testing you.

When you have doubts that you are *the one* then we test you and let your fears come in and we let you go down that road and path of doubt. You really know this deep inside yourself. We could not stop you from writing this book even if we wanted to. We could pause it, if you wanted to, but we couldn' do anything to stop it. We can't stop you from writing this book, we can't stop you from creating this magnificent life and from creating this mission, this is your mission. This is you as a SOUL who came in and said this is what you are going to remember and as a SOUL you were supposed to remember how to love and that is your mission. You are supposed to show the rest of the world 'How to Love'.

How you learned it was by going through all of these scenario yourself, the hurts, the deceits, the lies, the cheating, the abuse everything. You had to go through it to really grasp it. So now when you have gone through it and you have come out on the other side, you have shown the world that you know what you are talking about. You were there, you went through the abuse the humiliations, the bullying, being abandoned, not being loved, the ridicule, being alone and scared.

You tried everything, you were a single Mother, you were without a penny to your name.

Remember Mexico? You sold everything in Sweden and you left for Mexico with a ticket and two suitcases and only one suitcase made it to the end destination. That was a period that was very trying for you. You didn't have financial security but you believed in us and you jumped off the cliff because you knew you would be ok. We showed you how people just helped you two get to where you needed to go. After Mexico you two went to West Texas and Dennis wanted to show you his beautiful place and you loved it eventually but you felt it was too remote to stay so you went on a vision quest to ask your 'Universe' where you two were to go next and do you remember our answer?

How could I forget? I saw a sign with huge neon letters reading the word WASHINGTON DC with blinking lights and very colorful letters and I laughed because I knew you all did not want me to make a mistake so you 'spelled it out' very clearly so I could not doubt what we were to do.

It was not easy because Dennis did not want to leave Texas, but I could not see building a life out there in West Texas so he did what he felt he had to do and we went to DC. I was struggling with Dennis and his love issues. He had a special feeling about how 'love' was supposed to be and since he had been married several times before I knew I had to be the 'rock' in the relationship and be very adamant about not giving up on us. My patience and my commitment was put on trial almost all the time. He was pushing my buttons to get the 'usual' reaction he was used to with his previous wives but I was not 'playing' the game because I saw what was going on. Sometimes I lost sight of it but most of the time I knew what he was up to energetically and I was not participating in his game. He was used to controlling through energy but he had met his 'over-woman' and he knew it but still tried.

When Maa came into my life I felt connected again and my power
increased and I knew it was just a matter of time before he would see
that with me, life would never be the same.
There was a reason we met in Mexico when we did. I knew and he
knew it was not coincidence but life in DC was hard and losing sight of
'why' we were together was constantly happening.
I believe I would not have 'made it' if I had not experienced my
Grandfathers unconditional love.

His love was beautiful and for the rest of your life you were
more or less looking for that. Not until you met Sai Maa did
you understand what unconditional love was again. And that i
your whole life purpose to learn and to give. That is what Maa
was teaching you, that is what your Grandfather was teaching
you. Or could we say that is what Maa and your Grandfather
got you to remember. Here on Earth you don't really learn, al
you do is remember. Simple right? Well as you see it is no
always as simple as it sounds.

Your name means light. You are light you are love. That is your
mission. Animals, people and plants are naturally drawn to you
They are drawn to your energy. When you were 16 you looked
up and said, "When I am 36 I hope people will hear and listen
to my words".

I remember thinking that 36 was old and remember also wanting
people to be attracted to my mind not my body. Today I laugh at the
fact that we as youngsters don't always get it.

Don't worry dear that is exactly what's going to happen. You
are just a little more mature than 36 but you had to have your
children too because that love was important to you. And in the
end you will see that you have really been blessed that you
chose as an infant to survive.

You have blessed so many people by walking on this Earth. All the people you have helped and sent your love to has not been easy but when you look back at it, you know it was worth it. Get ready dear, your life is about to change and unimaginable events and places are going to take place. You can't even imagine it and you have a huge imagination like we keep telling you.

I have been told that throughout my life so it must be miraculous for it to be able to exceed my expectations.

Your life mission is *love*. To teach *love*, to be *love*, through your music, through your meetings, through your art, through your speech, you radiate love. When you are thinking of someone they will feel it. They will instantly feel it in their bodies. When they think of you they will instantly have a connection with you, because you will instantly be with them. Like we said You will have the vibration of Sai Maa. That's why Sai Maa said what she said when she said "Learn to Love. Learn to love your Husband. Most of all learn to love your Self."

I have heard it and now when the book is 99% finished I do 'see' it but it has taken a long time for me to grasp this. When I went to Sai Maa, she worked with me to get rid of so many obstacles I was carrying around keeping me away from total love and light. It is amazing the kind of life I am about to live and I feel so blessed. All I will be doing is radiating love.

Your love is stronger than anything and that is the reason why there are a lot of people that will want to get close to it.

Your job will be to guide people in the right direction, including Dennis. We put the highest belief in that you will do this and that you can do this. You will change people from all parts of the world and once you have touched people, the ripple effect will be happening and people will be tuning in and just opening up to that love. We didn't use Sai Maa because she is here for a different reason. We use you because that was your project. That is your process in the millennium. We could have used a lot of different types to do this task but you speak to people of all walks of life, the person that is working the fields, your next door neighbor, in fact everybody, not just one type of person you are able to connect with everybody on all levels.

The way you work and the way you feel for people is what we needed and like we say, we have no time to waste.

So it is a mission, it is not a Churchly mission it's a mission of love. And that transcends all other kinds of missions out there. Love, which is more powerful, is exactly the opposite of fear you will show the world how to live it.

Is this a session? Do you remember when I asked this question?

Yes we do, and yes this is a session. And yes we will teach you more. And yes we will raise your frequency more. We need you to do quiet time as well. So your cells can assimilate. So you can relax.

And be careful of your thoughts because they lead to words. As long as you are up on the high frequency you are fine. When you go down on the lower frequency your thoughts and word will go on a lower vibration, that's why we are connecting with you on the higher dimension, so you have to get up there.

178

We love you and guide you and will be with you all the way. We appreciate you from the bottom and the top of our hearts all that you are doing and you will be bountifully receiving our love.

You have our gratitude. Stay in your heart, and give with your heart. From all of us to you. We love you and have been following you and helping you and guiding you and now we are grateful, so grateful that you are realizing your mission on Earth, and from the sisters and brothers of Orion, we embrace you we love you and we see you already be enlightened faster than you can even think of. And when you see Orion, just know we are sending love to you.   May peace and love surround you, Amen. Love from Jesus, Oren and DaBen, Muhammed and Maa, Yoganandya and Buddha, we all love you, sending our love to you. And you know me Viva, so grateful. So loving so beautiful, so radiant, we love you. Our love is greater than you can imagine. We are so thankful, and love the fact that you are the Steward on this Mission. We believe we could not have chosen a better student/ mentor for this Mission.

Hmm.

You need to take the role of a spiritual leader. That is something you have to grasp and declare and then go into. So that is something we stress that you remember how to stay in those high levels and keep yourself cleansed at all times

Ok.

Sai Maa.

Do you remember the first time you met Sai Maa?

Yes, how could I forget. I was late coming to her 'gathering' and I did not know what to expect. A friend of mine, Anthony, had told me of her and that I should see her. I was not in a hurry and when I came to the hotel I understood I was late. I remember walking in at the back of the hall and when I opened the door to go in, I saw hundreds of people standing up with their hands in the air 'pulling' balls of energy into their chakras. Right when I came in Maa turned and looked right through me and I ducked behind some chairs in the back to not be noticed and while I was hiding there I knew she had seen me. remember feeling a bit awkward and then I found a seat. I remember the feeling of her looking right through me and it made me uneasy. also felt 'who did she think she was' and I realized that she had presented herself to me in a dream previously. When I was 'working on' a client who had cancer I remember asking my Universe how to work with this client to not hurt myself and I got the exact same lesson Sai Maa was teaching hundreds of people in this room. My mind was racing and wondering, "Who is she?"

Do you remember how you felt weeks after 'meeting' her?

Yes, I was irritated because she had gotten under my skin. She irritated me and I could not understand why. I just knew I couldn't forget her and my friend Anthony kept talking about her and telling me about the meditation sessions that were held in DC every two weeks. So I joined and started with a group of Sai Maa followers and meditated every second week with them. I enjoyed it. I was still skeptical of following someone. It didn't feel right. I had always listened to myself and my Universe and I felt that was enough but still I was curious about her 'Shakti' which I could feel when I meditated with the group.

I also knew she had 'come' to me in the dream and taught me another technique of healing which was very powerful. So who was she? Well all I could see was that people were drawn to her. I was watching her and as long as I felt it benefited me I continued to go. I was still seeking a lot of unanswered questions I had about what to do with my life and she seemed to help me find peace and power in myself. I felt she helped me empower myself and I could see she helped a lot of people with that as well. I met some wonderful people and kept contact with them.

I think she came to DC while I was there two times and I saw her at least one more time there and then my husband wanted to move to Texas and the doors closed for me to stay in the area so I moved with him. I was devastated for many reasons but one of the reasons was that I would not have my meditation group and then we talked about me joining them via skype and that made the move easier.

Do you remember when you went to see her in Vail?

Yes, my relationship was rocky and I was miserable and the DC group sent me money to go to Sai Maa. I was so thankful that they were so generous and I saw Maa. In front of 6-800 people she asked me "Why are you here? I cried and said my husband wants to divorce me.

181

She said, Thank him! I was confused??? Thank him for wanting to divorce me? Yes. Otherwise you wouldn't have been here. I see your point. I said but I was still uncertain and mad at him and very vulnerable so when she said to thank him I was perplexed. At the time I was emotionally at rock bottom, I could not get further down Economically I had not a dime to my name and I was not working and could not find a job I was trained to do. My degrees were worthless because it was too narrow, I am a film professional, and the jobs were either in NY, DC or LA.

Do you remember Sai Maa inviting you to go to her Journey of Profound Healing?

Yes she invited me in front of all those people and I understood that not everyone gets personally invited but I did not know where the money would come from but since I had gotten money from the group I felt there must be a way. I meditated to the universe and said if I am to go to Maa, you will provide for me. I knew that one film project could be enough so I turned my faith to the universe to provide for this if this was to be. I knew I would not get anything from my husband who wanted to divorce me.

You see we provided like you asked us to.

I know you did. But why?

Well that we don't have to tell you now, do we? You know 'we are YOU. You know we/ you needed to get rid of the baggage you had been carrying around stopping you from being that powerful 'divine being' that had created this mission of enlightening the world. We/you knew you needed a little help getting to this place a bit faster so we/you created the circumstances you needed to get a film project just in time for the next "Journey of Profound Healing" with Sai Maa.

And then off to be a week   with Sai Maa on the intensive Journey of Profound Healing to get rid of the 'stuff' around you and get you to shine like you did when you were born.

I remember the time before Sai Maa where I was struggling and now after the Journey of Profound Healing when I am flying. What she did in a week I had worked on for decades and was still not finished with. I feel such gratitude towards her 'work' that I can't explain it in words. To understand you have to do it for yourself.

That is my recommendation to all who read this book. With Divine Love, Helene

Wow, did you see that?

We wanted you to see the star.

What happens when a star falls? Has it died?

No, as you know nothing dies it just goes over to another form. But a star is like the sun.

Could the sun do the same?

Of course,

But then the sun would stop shining for the earth.

Yes, it will be in another form somewhere else doing something else and Mother Earth would be in another form doing something else, in another dimension. We mean everything is changing, the earth is changing, you are changing, you feel the thunder and lightening changing and that is true, that IS changing, the lightning is much lighter, that is true.

"Dear readers, whenever I am up in these dimensions and I ask questions and realize that some of these questions I already know the answers to but since we are barely touching many subjects I am going to keep my conversations here for you to read as well. When I am up in these dimensions I cannot recall most of the conversation and that is why I record it and then transcribe it afterwards. I want to keep this dialogue as authentic as possible and sometimes I feel the stuff we are covering is a bit 'out there' for many and for others it is no big deal but I still feel it is important to include it because it is my path and my experiences and my truth. With Love always, Helene".

How to get rid of fear..

When people read this book, how will it help them?

The essence, the beauty, the love will go to them. You will have a couple of examples of dissipating negative energy. You will also be showing how to raise the vibration and for enlightening like you do with the Gold/Silver/White vibrations.

Can people do what I do, like putting hearts around negativity and 'see' it dissipate?

Maybe they won't be able to see the negativity dissipate like you, but it will still work. We know it is difficult to understand that if they don't see it how will they know it works.

We are going to ask them to believe, ask them to try it. What do they have to lose?

Ok breathing all through the feelings?

Yes the breathing exercises. And then letting it go through the hearts.

Is everybody going to be able to do this?

Yes, that is how we are going to be able to get rid of the samskaras (stuff) around people by teaching them how to breathe through it.

They are going to be simple exercises because you have gone through books with too complicated exercises and said, "Ok I can't do this." It's got to be simple plain and effective. You are going to teach with your heart.

Breathing in the doubt and breathing it out with a heart around it, is another good way to do it. Breathe in negativity surround it with a heart and breathe it out and see it disintegrate. So there are many ways of doing it and you have already given some of the tools.

What you just told me here, are people going to be able to imagine it in their minds eye and see it dissipate like I am?

We are not sure how much most people are going to be able to see, but if you draw it and you show them how to, you will be able to help them visualize it.

How to get rid of fear and other negative feelings.

We want you to breathe through all of these feelings and love them.

What do you mean?

Breathe in the 'feeling' and love on the feeling as you breathe out, put hearts on it ☺ Send lots of love. Feelings of irritation breathe in, and then breathe out with love surrounding it. The fear? Breathe in, put a heart around it, breathe out. Imagine the word Fear, put love around it. See it dissipate or imagine it dissipate.

Wow, that felt much better.

That's exactly how you do it. You will be doing that in situations that are hard and harsh and difficult, you just breathe in the emotion and put love on it and breathe out.

Da Vinci and Jesus, Michelangelo and God.

When Da Vinci painted the 'Last Supper', what happened with Maria Magdalena?

> At first she was in the picture sitting beside Jesus. The churches did not want Maria Magdalena to be there so she was removed by them.

Did Da Vinci remove her?

> Yes, he needed the money and he needed to be in good favor with the elite so he took her out.

> The men were trying to take all the power and they knew that they would be able to keep the power if they didn't show her in a prominent position sitting beside Jesus. Having a woman sit beside Jesus would be too controversial and would not help men stay in power.

But in real life was she around Jesus?

> Yes she was.

Did they love each other?

> Yes.

Was she his wife?

No, not in a churchly way, but in his heart she was. And they felt that they were partners for life.

So, Da Vinci painted the painting with her and had to change the painting, but if you look closely you see that he left a space for her beside Jesus.

Interesting. What about the Sistine Chapel, the hand that touches God.

God is depicted as a man and in the Sistine Chapel you see the connection.

Michelangelo wanted to show that YOU (all of you) are the connection with God, it's not just Jesus. You are the connection, You (all of you) are the Rainbow Bridge, You are the ones that connect the 'Universe' with the Earth.

You are each connecting Divine Souls, so you are the ones with the power and when you believe that then YOU ALL are able to create. When you believe that you are/have the Divine Power you are able to create. So when you know in your Soul that you are Divine, you are creation, and that is what YOU Helene is going to be showing the world.

That is how powerful, you as human beings are. There is nothing, yes a bullet can kill you and then you will just go down into another human being or stay up on the higher dimensions but there is nothing that can stop you when you decide something. That is what you (Helene) are going to show the world. We are very happy that you are going into this subject because we never knew you were interested in this. You are waking up to the fact that you have always loved art but now you see it in a completely different way.

I went to art school, doesn't that count as interest? I am an artist and love doing sculpture and painting, doesn't that show I have an interest in art?

Yes, but we were thinking that we didn't know you were interested in the symbolism as well.

That is interesting you would say that because I am always projecting Sacred Geometry. Wouldn't that count for that? And in art school we learned about the symbolisms used by the artists through colors and symbols. I even bought several books on the subject...

Yes we agree.

If I were to draw like Michelangelo would you guys assist me?

Yes we will. You see that you are able to draw. You never thought you were that good but you are. We want you to see that you are able to do anything you want to do and if you want to draw like Michelangelo then we will assist you in doing that.

Hey, who doesn't?

Well, it's all up to you if you want to sing and write music like the best composers we will be there too, you just have to be up in the higher vibrations and then you will be fine.

I have seen that in action and it feels amazing ☺

A day in Helene's shoes:

Sometimes my day starts at 2AM, 5AM or 7AM all depending on what the 'Universe' has in store for me. I start my day by bathing in my bathtub with all kinds of essential oils to soothe my senses and cleanse myself and get me ready for meditation. Before getting out of the bath I send Loving hearts to my family and friends and to the people on my 'list' who need physical healing. I usually send the hearts to governing bodies of different countries to help resolve conflicts. Then I either get out of the tub and meditate for about an hour or stay and meditate in the tub. Then I 'connect' with the Universe and they transmit. I transcribe the transmission and then go on my day with the 'chores' they have set up for me to do.

Now almost all of the day I am editing this book so I don't have time to do anything else than write...

I make my raw juices for the day and eat spirulina, chlorella, maca and other herbs and drink lots of herbal tea.

I sometimes take a nap when the Universe is working on me/ updating me.

I take my dogs for walks and sometimes I reach to do some reading.

I write, I play my guitar, I paint and draw and I exercise and do the Five Rites or also named the Five Tibetans.

My life is pretty full of beautiful experiences and I am enjoying living like this. At times I need to see other people so I take a trip to the city and enjoy some afternoon tea with friends.

That's about it.

Dancing with Jesus

Should I tell them about my dancing with Jesus?

We think that's an interesting part because usually nobody dances with Jesus. Jesus is beyond everybody so we think that you can put that in there and we also think that after you dance with him, he tells you to go higher. Pointing upwards. And just leave it at that. We think that is a very interesting thing that has been happening with you. So we think that will be a very interesting part of the book. There is not that much that needs to be said about it. It's just that when you do your meditations that is what happens that's where you are.

On one of my meditations I needed to go higher and the Universe told me to look up towards the sky and then I saw some spiral steps that led upwards and I walked up them and when I had rounded the stairs I saw Jesus standing there and I walked over to him because I wanted to give him a hug, and he took me and swung me around. I thought it was so much fun so now when I meet him we dance a little bit.

I always get a smile out of that and I get such a wonderful feeling of joy. After we dance he points upward and I go higher. This world is so wonderful and magical it literally 'lifts' my spirits. I feel so blessed to be in this 'place' of my life and to experience this bliss.

As a little girl you were able to see it. You chose this life before you came into this body. You chose your hurts, your abuse your abandonment as a Soul you chose it and you have been living it.

For all who are reading this it is important to know that we all choose our path before we 'come down' on Earth. That is why we are all 'seeking' and some of us awaken to our 'calling'. So if this resonates with you then you know you are close and I will be there for you if you need guidance. I have known all my life that I have this mission and looking back I was on track almost all of the time but I needed to become fully aware to realize it.

In your past lives you have been great powerful leaders, female and male. In previous lives you have been a slave, you have been in dire poverty, you have also been a Native American and like you once said yourself, you believed that you have been practicing all the religions. In each one of your lives you have believed in different religions, you have tried them all so in this life you couldn't conform to any one of them because in this life you saw above the religions. You were able to see beyond the religions because you were on a higher vibration.

So this time around for you, religions were just like what people think TV is.

You saw through it. You saw through people and you saw through religions at a very early age.

Nothing could dupe you. Nothing could amaze you because you saw through it and didn't believe in it. You saw where most people wore blinders, but for you the veil was not there. You saw how the pastors couldn't even see through their own action, being in a role that had nothing to do with reality. You could see that they were trying to show people the way, but it is like 'the blind leading the blind' and that never gets good results. (No offense to the blind people)

The Leaders of the churches are not the 'way-showers' but you saw that. These people were good people and they tried to show people the way but it was all in their heads, they were not connected to the most important part, their hearts.

Their hearts were not in it and they were actually afraid. They were afraid if they didn't do it right people would stop going to their churches. As long as they keep people believing, people will go.

As soon as people stop believing they stop going so they had to make them go by force. The Catholic church created different doctrines to make people go to church at least once a year. It's a long story and we will not go into the details and it was based on fear. Other religions do the same thing. You could see through that. You saw through everything. You are getting back to seeing through it all again.

When we resonate with fear there can be no love. Fear is on a lower vibration and nothing good will come of it, you will see. So when there is fear, love will be missing and love is the highest vibration. With the vibration of love you create miracles here on Earth.

Some part of you acknowledges that all of these religions are good for some people because it keeps them in some way going towards the right path. The religions have been needed and that's why so many people have gone.

Yes I see that.

Many people are weak and don't look at things the way they really are or can't see them because they are not really aware, so they have a pastor or priest or whoever is the head of the church who tells them how to think about things. The 'leader' also tells them to learn things their way and to read the books that tell things in a certain way. You never believed in that because you always saw it as fake. Now there is an ounce of truth in all of these religions, but if you just live through your heart you don't need religions, you don't need the beliefs. You just need to go inside yourself. You are Superior, you are a superior Divine being, you do not need anything else.

Get in touch with your Soul. Feel it. See it and understand it. Understand that your Soul has all of the answers and you don't have to go anywhere else.

Go inside your Soul go inside *your-self*, go inside your heart that's where the answers lay. And you know this. You have had a difficult time explaining it because people are not aware. They think their whole life is outside of themselves and it's really inside. So that is the reason why it's very important to have the Ascended Masters and Jesus and the Gods and the Devas and Devitas and the Arch Angels and the Angels because it helps people get on the right path but that's not the end path, those are the helpers. We know it sounds weird when we say Jesus is helper, but he is, he is a helper of humanity. He is helping humanity see their own light, getting each human being to see their own light.

As you know Souls do not die, they go on to a different body or a different task in the Cosmos or in the Universe.

You have had many lives, not you as a body, this body is only having one life, but you've had many lives as a Soul and you have experienced many different things. These many lifetimes have gotten you ready for what you are doing right now in this lifetime. So what you are doing right now, you have been preparing for lifetimes, and it is a huge mission you are starting. Your mission is to awaken people to make them understand how things work and to make them empowered in themselves. When you all are empowered in your *selves* we don't need handouts from anybody, then you are able to create your own lives. You do not need to look towards anyone else to create these lives you want. You have it in your-*selves*, You have it in *yourselves* inside yourselves. Your life is an example of what you have experienced and where you are now but also what your Soul has experienced in different lifetimes because you are *you*, you have always been YOU. When you explain this to people they don't understand it and most people still believe that they have only one life.

I know, it is like in the 1400's when Columbus knew the world was round and most people still thought it was flat.

You better make the best out of *this* time, well you better make the best out of every time because every time you come down to a new experience. On the other hand you are the '*way-shower*' you don't stand up there and preach and judge and tell people they have to look at it this way otherwise you are out. That's not the way it works. There is nothing that says that if you don't do it in one way, you are out. Yes there are good rules to abide by, but the only rules to abide by, is your heart.

You see the emotional intelligence or the heart intelligence is all you need. When you are 'run' by your heart you will do the right things.

You will never do anything wrong if you are working through your heart.
So the religions and all the beliefs out there they help people believe that there is something but the most important thing is for people to actually be able to look inside them-selves.

That inner voice is the key to living a Divine life full of joy. Do you remember when you were in turmoil, when you were about to divorce your ex husband, do you remember that you felt that you were going insane, because your inner voice was being contradicted so many times? The fear and the darkness and the depth of your despair was huge. You couldn't think straight and you couldn't feel love. You went to your friend Lene, and you looked at her and you were so unhappy. Do you remember that?

Yes I do remember, oh my gosh I remember. I felt so guilty because had made the promise to my daughter that she would have a Father and a Mother until she was grown up. Well, I had not expected her father to be treating me like he did and cheating on me and in the end it was unbearable.

Yes and what was most unbearable was when you understood that he had been sleeping around the whole 18 years that you guys had been together. When you understood that, you wanted to get out of there but you were so ambivalent and you stayed

You tried and you tried because you knew that your decision to get out of there was going to affect your daughter and your son and that's why you stayed as long as you did.

When you were almost going under because you were able to see his mis-chiefs, we had to show you in paper form or physical form what he had been doing and you were looking at us and thinking ok I am not crazy this is actually really happening.

You were so much in denial because you wanted to keep the status quo of the family going. Well we can't say that you should have done it faster, which we believe you should have, but you had to go through it your way. Your soul put you up on a higher level so you were able to see that life. We know you made a sacred promise to us but we also knew you needed to get out of there and you did. You told your daughter that in your house no other man would be there while she was in the house. Well that's what happened. She left very fast. Your promise to us was sacred and we appreciate that and we love you for doing it but as you see your fear kept you there too.

Wow, I wanted to make sure that my kids were safe, my life came secondary.

Yes and we saw that and we saw that that is how it was, but you are going to have to change that because you are very valuable. You are going to be helping this planet in a huge way and its people. Being humble is beautiful but we also see now that you need to take back your power and you need to get in gear for this mission. But this mission has been something that you have been working on your whole life and many lifetimes. So it's not just something that came now. The difference between 10 years ago and now is that the veil is being lifted and you are there where you are supposed to be right now. You are experiencing the second part of your life, which is a very beautiful part of your life.

Your power and beauty lies in your heart. And for those who can see, they can see that in you. They can see the beauty, they can see the power, they can see the Divinity and they feel it. When they get close to you they feel it. We want you to know that you know that we are behind you in all that you are doing. Loving and being love goes for everyone, everyone that you meet, we want you to be love.

When you go to Sedona, you are going to meet people that are not going to know who you are but they are going to be in a state of need and we want you to put hearts around them and we want you to understand that there is hope out there. On your trip, just keep sending those hearts to everyone and everybody, especially New Mexico. There are a lot of people that are deficient in the heart area. Do you remember how that was? You yourself were very deficient in your heart area, You had become so depleted in your love for yourself that you were in despair and you were almost suicidal. You felt you were so lonely in your marriage. Many times you were on a very low frequency, do you remember how that felt. Do you remember how unhappy you were?

Yes I do remember!

You kept playing that everything was fine in front of your children. But you knew it was not and you knew something was not right. Your experiences, your despair, is what people are going through today. Remember that. Remember the fact that people are going through what you went through, everyday. The difference between you and others is that you knew that there was hope somewhere and you kept going and you kept fighting.

You know right now, you *are Love*, you radiate love you breathe love, you sing love, you paint love, you draw love. When you play music love comes out and your words heal people, you just need to look at people and they will be healed. And we need you desperately as you know,

When you go back to that time when you were in despair and you did not know inside or out. You did not know what to do and you had no feeling of any love coming towards you at all.

When you felt that the only thing that kept you up was your children and kept you going, you loved them and you saw their beautiful faces and you had to do everything in your power to make things work. You had them and that was a huge reason why you didn't go under because you loved them so much and you knew that they were dependent on you. We know right now that you can go back to that state of mind but you can't really feel it but you remember.

You are pure love now and all you know how to do is radiate love because you are so filled up with it. But at that time you were so deficient, not for the love for your kids, that never stopped, but the love for yourself. You were so deficient and everything you had you gave to your kids. You didn't care what it would cost, everything you had you gave to them.

When you work with your mission like you do and you go out to people you are going to have to understand that there are going to be people with very low energy levels that are going to come towards you. You are going to have to work with them and give them love, every one of them. Everyone is equal, you know that, and that is why when you come to places you see people come towards you and they look at you and you are a little afraid, give them a smile and send them love.

Don't be afraid just send them love. You are the instrument for love so give them that.

Vibrating on higher frequencies

We need you to master raising your frequencies to the highest level. Then and only then will we be able to lift the veil. That's the way to do it, you are doing it right now.   Breathe in the golden light from the crown of your head.

Ok, I am there. I think. I really don't feel I am having connection with you guys. What's up with that, why am I not having that? Have you guys left me alone?

You are on a higher vibration you are just not used to being up there, so you get a little distracted a little pattern that gets you to go down on a lower vibration when you get up that high. You go" No I can't really do that, can I?" Yes you can."

I feel nauseous.

Well, you are up on very high dimensions.

Can you tell me what dimension?

You are up on the 45th dimension or more. That's very high. We are getting you up there because we are soon letting you go into the world.

Soon we have to release this book into the world and release this energy into the world. It's a very high energy and it is an energy that is not on this planet yet and that is why you are feeling very nauseous when you are up there.

Thank you for healing everybody this morning. That works very well. They don't know why but suddenly they have so much energy and it's because of you.

Couldn't you give them the same energy?

No not unless they connect with us, but you can from the earth plain. As long as they do not see us, they don't feel us and then we don't exist for them.

Ok. I can't even imagine not having you in my life. It would be a drag.

The same thing is going to happen with your governments, your churches and a lot of institutions. If you (all of you) don't see them they cease to exist.

Wow. That would be an incentive to get people to stop watching TV like I have for years. I stopped watching the news because it was only negativity and if I need to know what is going on I glance at the Internet and check the headlines.

People go around in ignorance and believe the lies they are told. They run around with smiles on their faces but deep inside they are pretty unhappy and scared and run by fear. People are slowly waking up to the fact that life isn't the way they have seen it and those that are waking up and seeing are going to be the ones that will be the happy people.

Those that don't will be having issues with their health. Its either you wake up and open up your heart or you have health issues because with the powerful energy approaching the earth it is an energy of opening up of institutions, governments, money, banks, militaries. It's a time for opening up their hearts, opening up to love.

So who are the ones doing the chemical trails (Chem-trails), who are the war mongers. Are they the reptilians?

Yes.

Now tell me more about the reptilian plan… Is that something we should have in the book?

Yes,

Are they planning to ruin the Earth? It really looks like it if you look at it from my perspective. These people seem to be planning to control the people that live on Earth and deplete it and otherwise ruin it and then move on to a different planet.

Well, it's not as simple as that, yes they want to control the planet and yes they want to control the earth. They want all the power and they want people to be dependent on them.

They don't really want to destroy the planet per say, but they see what's happening and they see what their doing has done to the Earth and they are not sure that it's possible to save the planet at the rate the destruction is going.
Yes they have a plan B, which is a place to run to in case things get out of control.

They have a feeling that people are becoming too awake. Awakened people are detrimental to their plans. When people awaken and they start using their hearts, the Reptilians are going to diminish in their powers.

That's how powerful the hearts are. So now that you know that, you know your mission. You know you have to do this. You know that there is nothing that can stop you and we know that you know that. We are just saying that by you knowing that there is nothing that can stop you, you should be able to understand your power as well.

The Reptilian plan has been going on for centuries and for each century that has passed there has been more and more elaborate planning taking place.

The reason why it could continue is because most people have been in the dark ages but they are just now coming out and will awaken. It is daunting to see people not seeing this and really that is also your mission. You are the eyes of the people,

Ok.

You have got to use them.

Ok.

You are the eyes the mind and the heart. You are the instrument that is going to awaken the people to the fact that they have been duped and what they believe in is not reality, is fiction and yes we do want you to see the Matrix one more time because that was a very good story.

Ok, I have another question. Most people wear blinders, but not I. I have been able to see through people for many years and then I got the blinders on because I guess life took over and now the blinders are coming off me again and I am able to see again.

I have seen all my life but not always through clear glass. What about the people that have never seen? How will I be instrumental in their awakening and getting them to see this and not seeing me as the enemy?

Well that is another thing we are looking at. During your unveiling there have been a lot of small things that have come into place and we want you to know that is just because you have always had your eyes open (in this life time) and you have always had your heart open.

Many will wake up but of course not everyone. There are going to be a lot of people not understanding you and saying "What is this crazy person talking about?" On the other hand a lot of people are going to wake up and *get it*. They are just going to "get it"!

I really hope you are right, because otherwise I am in some deep s…..t!

So what about the people that resonate with the military, that want to go to war, that want to do this, and I have been one of them. Is that because they are reptilian?

No. many good people like you, who wanted to do this for their country joined the military. (You didn't join the Military but you wanted to and you grew up as a GI Brat) And when they get in there they see what kind of a place it is. They do not understand until they are too far in, and then they see there is nothing they can do.

Every time there is a line of command there is always going to be a reptilian on top who will dictate everything. There are good guys in between on the lower ranks but on the top there is mostly reptilian because that is what runs the world and that is the 'old' rule. The new 'rule' is coming and people with open hearts are going to 'take over'. They need you all to send hearts to the military. Surround all military bases and specially the Pentagon with hearts every day. Just like you do, Helene, on your every morning meditation we want all people who are reading this to include in their everyday practices to surround the Pentagon and military institutions with hearts. Can you imagine what will happen?

Yes I can. We will shine light on ALL corruption and the people that are open to love will be able to take over and that will happen very fast!! We need it NOW.

I am asking ALL readers who read this to spend one minute of your day to surround the Pentagon and other institutions where you want change, to surround these places with hearts and just watch what happens.

What do I do with HAARP?

You put hearts around HAARP.

This acid rain we are getting after the Chem-trails? What do I do about that?

Put hearts around it. Put hearts around the military bases. Put hearts around the planes. It will terminate it.

Tell me about the Chem-trails? I hear they ruin the Gulf Stream and jet stream and everything.

> We have spaceships here that are keeping an eye on what's happening. We are letting them have moderate success so they think that they know what they are doing, but we need you to understand that you can stop this.
> Remember the 'argon' dissipater that you saw on youtube?

Yes.

> That is something that everybody can build and get rid of the chem-trails with. We need you to write about this. We have told you about some of it. Dennis got one on one of his gigs.

> We need you to mention it for people to become aware. This book will not go into any scientific proof or discussions of anything like that, this book is to wake people up to the love and how the love can dissipate negativity and hate and fear Regarding the chem-trails they do (for the lack of better words) mess up the atmosphere. Like you hear right now, there are no birds chirping,

Wow, yes, I hear no birds, wow that is horrible!! That was what I was missing. I didn't understand it. It is a strange grayness, no clouds and no nuances.

The birds stop chirping. It's like pollution.

How do I get rid of it?

Put love around the area.

Wow.

We want you to write about if people are noticing the weather patterns and clouds are different. People can dissipate it and help it to go away, just send hearts to it, send hearts all around it.

That is wonderfully empowering…

So people CAN make a difference. If enough people think about it they can take it away and that's the same that happened with the 'coast to coast hurricane' when 2 million people turned a hurricane around.

Can you imagine what happens when 2 million people are thinking about dissipating the chem-trails with hearts, it will work too. Just the power and force of that many people thinking the same thing and just watch how fast it happens.

We want you to know that when we are talking to you about the military who think they have the weather under control and they think they are able to change the weather, well in the long run it won't happen, they will not be able to change the weather and it is not going to be so, but we are letting them think that they have gotten what they need. Right now you hear there are no birds. Just continue sending hearts.

Now the weather is grey and the wind is still. You know that is not normal.

You are in an area where there are a lot of military bases at least 5 bases with a lot of military stuff going on. Send hearts around the bases.

Yes yesterday I saw military planes.

Send hearts around the planes and everything they were doing. You saw it and it wasn't a coincidence. You saw the clouds yesterday and they were feathery.

Yes, they were different.

So you understood that the stuff was being put out there?

Yes I did.
It's almost like they are putting a lid over everything so nobody sees what they are doing,

Well that's partly what they are doing. Surround them with hearts.

 Why haven't people come onto this idea before? Why does it come with me?

Well it's because you asked for it. This is part of your mission nobody else's.

Ok, I guess I have to be careful with what I ask for….

The difference is you are making a huge impact on the world. We are all going to have to be there to work with you. You see there are a lot of us up here, looking down and seeing what you are doing. We know you are happy about that and we also know you are tired of it and you want this to get going.

But there are a few more things you need to go through. You can't just do the talk, you need to do the walk and yesterday we revealed some of it. You have to be able to control your thoughts. No negative thoughts can come from you; they all have to be positive. Continue working on that.

Well there is something I want to ask you guys. You told me that we are one but you won't be like me and I won't be like you. But I am still one with everything and I am one with you guys too?

Exactly!!

Yes and I still don't understand it.

We told you that you will understand it when the veil has been completely lifted but until then you have to be 'cramming for those exams' until we say stop and you have arrived. So just jump right into it. That is all we can say. We can't really do anything up here until you have done what you need to do down there!

Understood…

I am working with the Pentagon, I am working with the White House, I am working with the Capitol, is there any way I can thwart the negativity by going in and looking at what they are doing?

No.

The only way you can thwart anything is by sending love and light. That's the only way. You can know the bills and everything and the physical part but you need to be on the spiritual level, the heart level. That's where you can do most 'damage' and good of course. When you send heart energy people that want to do negative 'stuff' will be stopped.

So even though I would have access to their meetings and stuff, all I can do is spread love?

YES.

I would like to have access to what Obama says behind closed doors not in the public, but what he believes.

You are right on the money. He is more Arab than anything else and he is working with the Arabs, he is working with the Arabs to ruin the US. He doesn't have any love for the US. He is working to ruin the constitution, he is working to ruin the American people. But he is just the puppet.

Oh my God, that is what I have thought all the time.

You have been right on the money from the day he started running for president. You already saw everything. You said Oh my God, this is horrible. You saw it right away.

But my spiritual friends didn't see it.

No, because you see what all don't see. You don't understand what you see, you see the truth, nothing but the truth, so help you God because you are going to need it. In every situation you can look right through people but, you can be blinded by people close to you because you are emotionally attached. The only way you can help is through the spreading of hearts, through love, that is the only way you can help.

What will it take for people to cease being corrupt?

With your love they cease to be corrupt that's why when you see a cop, send them love.

Can we all do this?

Yes, the more love you all send them the less corrupt they will be.

That is mind-boggling. I can imagine how powerful we all could get and turn this ship around just by love...Wow.

When you were up in a higher dimension when you were doing your practices and you get that light, that very high strong light. At that high dimension you take off. It's beautiful. And we want you to learn how to stay up there. Just remember how you did as a child.

I feel so lucky, I feel so loved, I feel so much love. I am in such a beautiful place. I am so lucky to have you guys. I really am appreciative of all that you have done and are doing with me.

It's such an amazing journey, experience, life. I wish everybody would experience this. Oh my God this is so beautiful. I am in love with life. I am in love with every single little atom, every single piece of dust. I just see beauty. It's so beautiful around here. I want everybody to experience this. Our heaven is here!! We don't have to do anything to go to heaven we just have to be. It's so beautiful and there is no explanation. I am here… I am in heaven. I love. I am. I am love. I am beauty. I am wisdom. Every cell of my being is love. Hmmm. I am love. I am in love with love. It's so beautiful. Oh wow this is bliss. Oh wow. I could stay here forever.

Dear reader, now seeing this little chapter I realize you are not able to experience even though I wish for you to. I just want to tell you that to experience this state of being is life changing and this would never have happened if I didn't continue meditating every day. I am so grateful for this(gift).

What Dimension is Earth in?

Most of Earth is in the 4th and 5th dimension. But a lot of the wars are still in the 2nd and then there are still many on the 3rd.

What about peoples' ascension?

> They are ascending to the 5th and 6th dimension. That's where most people will end up. They will need a catalyst and the catalyst is you. You will spark the flames and get it going.

Tell me why the churches are going to be falling apart?

> We believe that when people wake up they will see that they will not need the churches, they will come up on a higher dimension than the churches.

They will be able to see the churches with all the 'fear' and 'sin' and manipulation that has been going on and with their open eyes the truth will reveal itself.

That's a lot of people.

Yes, it is happening as we speak. People are not talking about it, but it is happening as we speak. So you are right on time.

Gosh, I feel it is so late.

No you are right on time. Everything that is happening is happening for a reason. You are here for a reason. There are no coincidences.

You do understand your mission is right around the corner and you are almost there. We want you to understand you are guided all the way through this. You are not alone. We do feel on some level you are in a vacuum, you are looking at this from the outside not really that you are inside it yet. And we also understand that you don't understand what's about to happen. You are doubting, please look into it. Look at it. There should be no doubt.

How will I be able to keep my integrity when people are going to be looking at life from their perspective, they will be looking at it with the perspective of 3rd or 4th dimension perspective and I am at a much higher perspective.

Don't worry about that. You need to project your true self and your true integrity. When you project that then you will be able to love unconditionally and they will get it.

I believe they will also resonate on a higher level when they go into their hearts. I will be helping all resonate on higher frequencies because that is needed to ruin the prevailing military and governments so the love and light can shine through. People have much more power than they are made to believe and just by sending hearts and love bubbles around the Pentagon they can dissolve negativity....wow that is amazing....

> Regarding the frequencies, well that is your weapon, and that is the reason you can't be having negativity and going down in frequencies, because you are going to have to be above these frequencies.

I remember reading James Redfield, The Celestine Prophecy and in one part of the book he was being chased and he had to learn to shift his frequency to become 'invisible', now I understand what he talked about.

> You see we understand what the military is out to do and doing right now. By you being able to go above and beyond the frequencies then they lose power and that is why we are stressing for you to be on such high frequencies. Because when you are above the frequencies their frequencies cannot touch you. You need to be in the frequency of love all the time.

> The frequency you are in right now makes you untouchable when you go down in doubt you become touchable. So your survival is by being up in the high frequencies. So it doesn't matter what happens to you when you will be up in those frequencies they cannot touch you. With the hearts and with the gold silver white lights and your frequencies you can ruin their machinery, by your frequencies you can ruin what they are working on.

Ok what about people that are on a lower frequency?

> Yes they are going to be having a hard time. When they
> meditate and they open their hearts they are going to be able to
> raise their frequencies too.
> You see. What you have seen in these last movies is what is
> possible from the illuminati and that's what they are working
> on. There is one thing that they cannot do, they cannot fight
> against the love energy. If there are enough people on earth,
> showing their hearts, the illuminati cannot fight against that.
> Their machinery and technology and everything like we told
> you before, will not work as they are planning for it to be
> working when YOU all unite your hearts.

Wow, that is self empowering to know that we as a people can together
ruin the plans that the reptilians have in store by uniting all of our
hearts. I almost feel like going to the Pentagon and meditating there
and sending love to all. I wonder how many people will join me.

> We are sure you will have many people wanting to change this
> state of what is going on and so when you declare that you will
> be going to the Pentagon and meditating we will see many
> people joining you. We just need you to finish this book first.

I know and I will.

Wow I saw that! How beautiful.

> Exactly, that is the way you will be seeing people on the other
> side. We made you see this with your 3rd or 1st eye, somebody
> who is not related to you. You will be able to see people on the
> other side here too.

You will be able to see what the president is up to. You are going to be able to see things that you normally would not be able to see and when you are up in those very high vibrations you are able to access of course the Akashic Records but there are more records you can access that are beyond the Akashic Records. A lot of people are going to be able to access the Akashic Records, but you are going to be beyond the Akashic Records. Where you have instant information, just like when people are thinking about you you are instantly there helping them and they feel you right away. You are going to be able to go beyond remote viewing which you are able to, and have been doing for decades, that is nothing new to you, but you will be able to view them and see exactly what is wrong with them right away.

It is difficult to do this with your own family because you have your emotions tied up to them but with other people you will be able to do it and you are able to do it now but you don't know this yet.

Your evolvement also happens to the people around you. You children, your dogs, your grandchildren, everybody you are connected with evolves when you evolve. Your parents both your sisters and your brothers. They don't know it but they are connected with you so they evolve as well. So your evolvement helps people too, especially those who are close to you.

The "Veil".

Dear Viva, Sai Maa, Yogananda, Buddha, Nithyananda, Muhammed Christ, Universe, Angelic beings, I am asking you all to tell me the truth, everything I have been doing in this beautiful life, has it been bunch of hogwash, is this just a fantasy that will never happen?

I want you guys to really answer this one. Is this book that I am working on and writing, is this just in my imagination that it will be a success? You see that could just be inside my mind that I am hearing this.

No, it IS going to be a success. We are behind you!

You see, again that could just be my freaking imagination or just my wishful thinking. I just want it to happen so it is going to happen? Right?

Right!

Is that the veil??

YES.

Because I want it to happen it IS going to happen???.....sssssshhhhh. Is that all you guys are telling me? Because I want it to happen it IS going to happen?

Yes, THAT is part of the VEIL!!!!! You are creating it.

What about these people that you have already lined up at Hay House that are ready to take it and so on and so forth? What about the feeling with me being one with everything so that I can see the path?

Well you have the instruments to see it now. You will make it happen.

Well you guys already told me this before.

Yes but you were not ready to accept it, you still wanted to be a little bit in your dream.

Ok, it feels like an anti climax, right now. It really feels like I have been talking to myself the whole time and ..

Yes, you have!!

What? That is NOT funny. What significance is that going to have with anybody reading this book? They are going to look at me as if I am a lunatic. I have just been talking to my- self, for my-self, about my-self. Doesn't everybody talk about themselves and talk to themselves? Well I don't mean all the time. Are you saying that when my inner voice and outer voice are one, that is when the Veil has been lifted.

Yes.

I have this feeling of anger and disbelief right now and I think I am going to have to digest this one.

We know you will.

This morning you are understanding why negativity comes into your life. You understand what happens when you let doubt take 'over'. The reason is because you didn't do what you were supposed to do every day. To keep your doubts at bay and keep you on a high frequency, you have to do what you are supposed to do every day for you to stay up there, it's as simple as that.

Wow, you mean if I had done the 5 Tibetans and created my drawing yesterday, like I was supposed to, I would not have had these thoughts? If I had listened to my 'inner' voice then I would have stayed on the higher vibrations

Exactly!

Wow, I am totally getting it.
If I am not doing it, I feel guilty and guilt brings in the other crap and I go down on a lower vibration?

Yes

Now I get it. Now I understand. That's how I have kept myself procrastinating all this time.

Yes.

Does that work for everybody?

Yes, if they don't follow their inner voice they don't get up on those higher realms. The 'inner voice' is the 'consciousness' or in other words the 'truth' and when you go against that, you go against the Divine flow.

Ok, I got it. I guess it took me a while to figure that one out.

Well you are still remembering.

Wow. So I definitely have a motivation to keep doing this every day. When I wanted to meditate every day prior to this, I had to force myself to do it and I would be 'good' for some time and then I would start slacking. Then I would meditate every other day and soon I was not meditating at all and feeling guilty about it, and that in turn made me feel bad and so on and the result would be that I would be on the lower vibrations and not be experiencing synchronicity. For the last almost 650 days I have not had one single day without meditation and I feel that is a huge accomplishment and I thank you guys for that.

We are thanking YOU for that.

Your awakening is something we see as very important for mankind. Through your book people will get an insight into how it is for the veil to be removed. How the world is closed and then suddenly how it opens up and how you are able to see everything on a much higher dimension.

Well your story is a story of staying on the journey, keeping yourself going, living in love and in the beginning it was looking for love, but living in love, giving love and for-giving. Always seeking for the Divine guidance and listening .

When they read my book and they are on the 3rd dimension or the 4 and I am up there telling them stuff from the 45th dimension, will the understand?

Not completely, just like when you read Conversations wit God.

You were reading it but not totally understanding it but you were opening up to it. And usually people who read your book have read these kinds of books before so they are open to the fact that they won't know everything and they won't question, they will gradually open up themselves.

Days later....

If you declare that you are that, then you ARE. That is how powerful you are right now.

That is true. But how many people are doing that right now?

Exactly, but YOU are. And when you are not mad at us, you are feeling it, you are understanding it and you are seeing what you are doing and it happens like you 'imagine' it.

I just want to 'en-light-en' people why I was mad at 'the Universe'. It has to do with how 'they' see things on the 'Spiritual plane' and how it differs from what actually happens on the Physical plane. Like you were saying, I was only mad because I didn't understand your perspective and now when I do, I am not mad anymore I feel that I have been 'en-light-ened' so that is another way to 'lighten up' ☺

You are our most precious being that is walking on this Earth. You do not understand it and we understand that you don't. And that is why you are in this humdrum of a period, you want to get out you want to get this finished, but on the other hand you are a bit scared of going deep into it.

I would like to go deep into it. I just don't know how and the information is profound.

We would like to show you. Remember the crop circles? That is our way of giving information to the Earthlings about what we are about to do. You project those messages as cards in your living room and you are sending that out yourself. See, without really understanding it, you are already sending out these vibrations to the world. And you do not think *you* are the *one*?

Yes I do and I know at least part of me knows that I am the *one* and the other part of me is fighting that and saying how that can be true. How can I be the *one* I have not always told the truth, I have not always been authentic, I had times when my heart was hurting and I have hurt others. I have not always said the best things and not reacted in the best way. When I have been stressed I have exploded. I have been very human, not always Divine, like you guys are telling me that I am.

At the same time I also feel I am Divine like you say.

Well you do remember coming to Sai Maa and saying, "Who does she think she is"?

Yes, I do remember and yes, that is part of my ego, I guess.

Yes, that is part of your ego but that is also part of you heritage. When you see someone like that, walking up and down the isle and having that many people coming to see her wondering what she has that you don't. Well the only thing she has is that she remembered her mission a little bit earlier than you did. She didn't have the baggage to get rid of, like you did. She grew up in total love. If you had grown up living with your Grandfather you would have been in complete love as well,

but you had already chosen your path before you came down to Earth so you had to go through what you went through,

Your experience in your life is how people are going to resonate with you. You have been there, you have done the stuff you have walked the walk. You are not just talking, you have actually been through it and that is the most important part of this whole thing. You have been through it, and come out on the other side. You see that is the big difference and of course also the fact that you do remember your journey. You remember it, you remember all the mistakes that you made, you remember the guilt, the feeling, the abandonment. You remember everything you have done and you have lived it. It was your experience.

Ok, how will I be able to show people that they are creators? How will I show them about the inside and outside integrity? I have witnessed what my energy does to people on lower frequencies and most can't handle it. They don't know what is happening to them until afterwards when they feel 'the plug' is pulled.

How will my teachings help people when they are on a lower frequency and I am on this high frequency? I had a hard time believing that I was a creator before I got up on these frequencies. Even though Winston Churchill did say that, "You create your universe as you go along." I remember that quote was something that stayed with me. I could understand it on an intellectual level but not entirely on a feeling level. It didn't completely resonate with me.

Exactly…that's what this whole book is about. It's not going to resonate right away with everybody who reads it but everybody is going to get a part of it and they will be learning bits and pieces and then go on with their lives. Just like when you read 'An Autobiography of a Yogi' by Yogananda. In the beginning you didn't get half of it but now you understand it from his perspective because you are there, you are above that but you are there.

Even though you didn't understand all of it right away you still read it. Remember you kept picking it up and re-reading it.

Yes I remember. I still pick it up and open a random page and re-read it. I feel I always get some 'new' information that helps me on my continued journey.

That is what is going to happen with your book. It's a very simple book, but the messages and the teachings are not simple, you know that, but it's simple to read.

To walk the path in someone else's moccasins that has been there and done that is what you are trying to get them to do. For them to understand your path and your journey while they are not able to have your moccasins on or your insight will not be easy, but they will be picking up your book like you did with Yogananda's.

We like the fact that you were really excited about your book and when you got excited about your book you couldn't fall asleep and you were healing all over the place and that energy was really going through you, it was fantastic. Well that is the energy we want you to be in because that is the energy of love and light and pleasure and beauty so you were feeling yesterday you just felt your body! WOW.

Yes I know and when I was healing people, I felt it was MUCH stronger.

Yes and you did because you were coming from an even higher frequency than you have been and you were feeling happy that this is happening.

This is really happening so we were just really charging you up with all that other beautiful energy we have been waiting to give you so that you can be there and be IT.

Your job (again for the lack of better words) is to be 'The Way-Shower', your purpose is to show by your example how to ascend and how to be up in these very high energies. When people read your book they are going to be seeing and feeling it, they are going to get bits and pieces. They are not going to get the whole cake at once but they will get bits and pieces of your whole life. But your mission is to show people how to empower themselves and see how far they are able to go in love.

Now to go from there and get back onto your path that you started lifetimes ago is not an easy task. You know it because you are having a hard time because you have a lot of things you are going to have to let go of.

You have to let go of a lot of beliefs that you had. You have to go back to the pure essence that you were. That is the big step that you are taking right now and that is the reason you have to go to the depth of yourself and your soul and change to make that the way you are supposed to be living. You have to accept it, you have to acknowledge it, you have to be it. You cannot just say Ok I will do it today. No, this is a lifetime commitment so you are having to shed some stuff that still is lingering around in order for you to wake up completely and to become completely authentic. So for you to get there you see what is happening. You see how your life is going to be changing; you see it already on the outside. When you are letting go you see already on the outside what is happening (someone bought the next piece of land) because that's what you have done, you have done it from the inside first, you are letting go. And yes you will have a small amount of … "oh, I don't want to let that go", but on the other hand you are going to have to let go. Letting go is going to make you feel so free. Now, if there is any fear left, that definitely has to go.

That is something you cannot be carrying around at all, that is something that has to go away. Fear is your enemy, which means you cannot have fear and love in the same place at once so you are going to have to let go of fear for love to be completely there.

You see that is one of the reasons you have to be able to control your thoughts, all of your thoughts. That is one of the reasons why you have not been given the last part of the veil because you could become a disaster for people by your thoughts. We see you are controlling them but not all the way.

If you hate somebody you could be saying, even silently, I wish this person is dead and the problem is that is what would happen.

So you really have to control your thoughts. Until you are there we are not able to give you the last part of the veil. So now you know what you are going through. You see how your thoughts create your reality.

Earlier today you were very down and very unhappy because of this neighbor that was building something close to your house you were really down and getting all negative. At the same time you had issues with Dennis and then you said, "Ok. I am going to take a bath and cleanse and I am going to be fine!" Wow look what happened? You took a bath and you are back at your work and when you look at the two problems you see them as small stuff, not getting to you. You see that's how you get rid of all negativity, by just cleansing and continuing with your life and your path.

Will you guys be here to guide me?

We will always be with you, we will not leave you, that is the truth. You just have to own your path and be it.

You are upset you didn't believe you would be able to do it, but we think you have come back and understood that it is still possible, you are not as sure but you still see it as a possibility and when you talked to Helen yesterday and she told you that she changed a price of the course just by thinking it, we heard and we felt you thinking about the fact that you can do the same thing with the book. We are very proud of that because we believe that you understood that.

So, here we are. You have had most of the veil lifted, you understand it is all about YOU and up to YOU to do this and we will stand by you and aid you, just like we said we were going to from the beginning. The difference is you are very clear about the fact that it is YOU that is doing this and that you are being aided by us.

BTW Did you see you saw Dennis through the wall behind you, walking the dogs?

Yes.

Well you are able to look forward and see 360 degrees so we want you to start practicing that. You can already do that but you just didn't know it. We just made you see it.

The only difference is that I think he was supposed to have an orange shirt on and he had a blue one. I am not sure what I saw.

You weren't looking at the shirt, you were looking at the sun coming on him. Yes it was a bright sun and that is what you saw.

Wow, I thought that was fun. I did see what I never knew I could. It sometimes feels like I am taking baby steps.

Osho says to live as if you are the first ones on Earth.

I guess it would be profound to see things through the eyes of someone who first came upon Earth. Just before writing this book I had a profound experience walking down to the river with my dogs. It was as if I was 'seeing' the grass and trees along the way for the first time. They had a glow and their colors were much brighter than I had ever seen them. The green was so beautiful that I was in tears at the profound beauty.

> Yes we remember you walking that time, only you did not have your dogs with you. We were there when you experienced this. You were up on a higher dimension and you could feel the trees and grass and you communicated with them as well.

Yes I remember that and it was profound. It took me by surprise because I had taken that walk many times but never 'seen' it or 'felt' it like that. I went many times in hopes to 'see' it again but the experience has not repeated itself.

> Well you could have the same experience now because now you are in the light 99% of the time and if you are not you just call it to you. We would suggest you go and take a walk and experience it again.

Really? Ok I will take you up on it and do it again. I can't wait.

I went out just to connect to the Earth and it was magic. When this book is finished I will take you up on it.

"Once you make a decision, the universe conspires to make it happen."
Ralph Waldo Emerson

> This book is a story about YOU, but like you know YOU are just a part of the 'Universe'. You are just a part of everybody so look at it like that and see it as a way to enlighten the masses by telling your story and we will be by your side always.

> With this book you are going to be helping your neighbors, your countrymen, your Earthlings, your fellow animals and plants just by sending love to everything. Isn't it beautiful?

Yes it is and I see more beauty where it comes from.

> We are pleased you are writing about your life as well. That is the essence of the book. Through your life story you are showing people your truth and the way, so continue writing about your life and when it is possible put in the Divine guidance that has been with you throughout your life. By doing so you are telling people what they see and feel is real. The red thread through everything is that you have been divinely guided and most of the time you have listened.

Yes I agree. Except for when I have not and have been human and done it my way.

> You are going to be telling your story so people understand who you are.
> It is very important people understand who you are.

Why do they need to know who I am?

You have to understand that people need to hear and see and feel you. They need to see and read about who you are. So yes you will be writing your story.

Ok what about the space ships that are my allies? How are they going to help me and when? How will I connect with them?

That is another part of the veil. When the veil is gone you will see that you are connected with them a lot and have always been. Right now you don't see that you are connecting with them and that they are assisting you in many ways.
You know *we are all one*.

Oh gosh, the '*we are all one*, phrase' I missed that one, laughing… I love the fact that we are all one.
It's just that you guys can see me but I can't see you. That's not fair.

Well the only way you can see you is through the mirror. When you look in the mirror you see you and everything too. When the veil has been lifted you will be connected, physically you will see it, you will see the light beings and the space ships and the UFO's and us and everybody. Right now we are getting you ready to see everything on a physical level.

Will I be freaked out?? (I say that smiling, because I have always, or at least I feel I have always said…'Universe take me up there'.) Again we all have to be careful of what we wish for, because it becomes true! We ARE creators of our lives ☺

We are preparing you.

Ok.

Should I talk about the reptilians in the army?

Yes you should.

Hm.

What if an army man comes to me and complains about his boss?

You will tell him. Send hearts. Send love. Surround your loved ones with hearts and you're your enemies as well. That is all you can do with these people. That will destroy the reptilians.

Really?

Yes,
Reptilians are a construct, which means they are not natural in the sense that we talk about natural.
They thrive on energy from negativity. The more negativity the more reptilians there are.

What about the Kings and Queens and the Royals?

Yes they are reptilian and they are the largest of them. They want to keep people in ignorance fear and poverty. As long as they can keep people in that they will prosper. Now like we said with Helen, reptilians cannot have love. That is one of the reasons why when Diana came to the Palace, she had a hard time with the Queen Mother and with her husband Charles. They are both reptilians. She came with all this love and her light shone so bright that they were becoming second hand to her. That is actually what happened.

231

You saw it yourself, when Diana came to the palace, the public's attention went to Diana, not the Queen or Prince Charles. Without Diana they have restored it somewhat. Kate is not reptilian and William is like his Mom, and he has his Dads genes but it is not enough, he has his Moms light. They are trying to put Charles and his mistress Camilla to head the throne. Those two are reptilians. We think that is not going to be a good thing. If they do that we believe it will be the end of the Monarchy. They are not going to be a popular Monarchy. They need to put William and Kate as the heirs. Those two need to be there for the kingdom to continue, which is what we believe.

I remember Diana's glow. It was visible on all the photographs.

Yes Diana's light was shining light on all the things that were negative in the palace. And that is also a reason she was alone and not able to do this.

When you shine light on the reptilians they will diminish. Enough of us shining lights on them and we will not have the governments and the police force that we have today or the military that we see today. So it's all about making sure the love is flowing freely.

Ok I feel there is something you are not telling me.

Well they are not used to 100% love.

They are used to the lack of it so how can that destroy them.

It will destroy the negative side of them, even they can be changed into positive people.

Wow then they need a lot of love?

That is true they need a lot of love.

Just like I send love to the Pentagon every day? A lot of love is what they need.

What about the 'Spaceships' should I write about them as well?

Of course you should write about the Spaceships. They are here to help humanity. Everything we are telling you, you should write about.

Most of the Spaceships and the UFOs are your allies; they are around you all the time. You have seen them and they protect you.

Yes they don't scare me anymore. I see them like I used to when I was a child. I guess the veil is gone because I see them again.

They are keeping a close watch on what is going on with Mother Earth. They come down to help you and make sure you don't destroy yourselves. They are friendly and want you to survive because then they can create more places like Planet Earth in the universes.

They are going to be helping you create what you need to create.

That is wonderful

The Peace sign turned the right way according to the dream I had a couple of years ago. It looks different in black and white. To see it in color go to my website...**www.helenevgross.com**

Dear ones I was thinking about my art 'The Peace Sign' turned the right way that I created over two years ago. I saw in my dream that one of the reasons we have wars is because what we use as a 'Peace Sign' is actually a war sign. And what I drew was how the sign should be turned like a tree with 3 branches turned upwards. This is important because we need to get this 'Peace' going. Do you have any suggestion for me my dears?

We agree 100%. You need to have a picture of this in your book to emphasize how the sign should look like. When the population runs around with a false peace sign it is no wonder there has not been a stop to the wars.

Who do you think was behind the dream?

Well I don't wonder anymore. I am so used to you guys 'putting' things in my head now. It would be awkward if you didn't.

We know and we appreciate you listening.

Wow, I almost can't believe the growth I have done in this short period of time. In almost one and a half years I have finished this book and I have grown 'spiritually' what it takes lifetimes to grow.

Well you have been at this for lifetimes.

Yes, but I mean it has gone very fast in this lifetime. Right?   Please make me feel good about this…

Yes we have been speeding up your growth so you can go out into the world on a very powerful level and also so people can see and feel your evolvement.

I hope people can follow my back and forth evolvement and understand this dialogue is an ongoing dialogue between you and I and that it is not easy for me to 'grasp' the truths that I was 'remembering'. When I re-read my book I can see the parts that were from the beginning of my writing and those towards the end. It is almost 2 different people, the before and the after. Even though we know there is no such thing as time. It is all now.

We believe that when they read it they will 'get it'.

I want to mention what happened to me when I surrendered to the 'Universe'. Up till that point I had very strong beliefs in myself and at the same time I was 'fighting' the inner 'demons' regarding my 'spiritual life' versus my 'physical life'. I realized that I needed to stop fearing what would happen if I led a 'spirit' driven life. I had already tried the 'physical' go get a job and join the 'Rat Race Life' and then keep going and it wasn't working for me even though I tried.

You do remember the moment you finally said," I surrender!"

Yes, I was at a Vail Retreat (this sounds better than it was, I had no other choice than to surrender) with Sai Maa and I was very committed to change and I wanted to thank Sai Maa by writing in her guest book and those were the words that came out. Surrender and Grateful!!! That was how I expressed myself.

We were so happy you had decided to change your direction and we are happy you are nearing theend of the book so you can really combine the Spiritual remembering and the Physical writing your experiences and then going on tour with the book Yayyyyyy

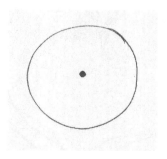

The Seed of Life

Is it the end?

Yes dear ONE, you are at the end of this book, but this book is just one of many to come. Remember you will be living many years on this planet.

You have a lot of work ahead of you and with the help from your fellow humans you (all of you) will turn this 'ship' around and understand that your Mother Earth loves you. She needs your cooperation and love to do this. Mother Earth will help you all evolve if you just 'tune into' her. If you have the time to sit still and listen she will 'talk' to you and fill you with love energy ☺

So continue enveloping hearts around your property and all people and animals you meet. In the mornings when you say Good Morning to someone surround them with hearts. We love you all, feel the love vibrating from this book. Have it near your bed and you will feel the energy. From all of us up here to all of you on planet Earth we send you our deepest love from the bottom and top of our hearts to all ☺

Thank you and sending hearts back at you!!!

Dear Readers/Co-creators,

I want to thank all of you for being part of my experience, and I can't wait to meet you all in person. One of the reasons why we incarnate on this planet — is to experience and to love.

To my dear loving children I want to thank you for giving me the chance to love you and for loving me even though I was not perfect. I believe you guys saved me from a lot of grief just by being yourselves and by radiating such beautiful love. Without you I would have been lost many times.

You gave my life meaning and by your presence you kept me grounded even though I had gone through some harrowing experiences. Your presence made me 'fight' for a better life and not give up until I had achieved it. I am eternally grateful that you walk on this earth and feel blessed that you chose me as your Mother. I will love you eternally.

To my dear Mother and Father I want to thank you for giving me life. Without life I would not have been able to have this beautiful experience. I am eternally grateful for the experience of the lack of love and for the experience of abandonment that you gave me and without that I would not have had to search for the love and security throughout my life and I would not have been in the beautiful space I am now.

I thank my ex husband who gave me the experience of rejection and infidelity which made me look for true unconditional love even more intensely. Without that experience I would probably have 'settled' and not experienced these last years magical writing of this book. I would not have experienced a life 'in total love', like I have now. I don't leave the 'state of love' I AM LOVE all of the time. I don't ever feel the 'lack of love'. Wow what a beautiful transformation!!!

To my beloved friends in many countries I am deeply grateful to have you in my life. You know who you are. Thank you for the encouragement and the 'help' you have given me throughout my life and through writing this book.

To my dearest Sister B, thank you for being there for me even though what I told you was not what you wanted to hear. I love you always and wish you the best.

To my dearest Brother A, I know you doubt some things but I hope you understand that this is a gift in the end and all of us had agreed upon this before we entered. love you always.

Dear Suzi....wow I can't even begin to explain how you amaze me with your skills. Thank you for helping me on tour and for being the 'pitbull' and for your amazing talent in getting us to the nicest places and seeing that we are treated nicely. I would travel with you anywhere. I am so grateful to have you in my life.

To my dearest Kiwi Sister Helen, your encouragement and love and unbelievable belief in me throughout this process and your passion and 'no-nonsense keep on going' attitude made this book a reality.

I am so thankful to have you in my life and I love you dearly and cherish our sisterhood!!!!!

To my dear husband Dennis, thank you for putting up with me during my writing endeavor for the last two years. Your support has been invaluable. Thank you for continuously pushing my buttons so I continue to grow. Thank you for the magical music you create and for your love.

Helga, thank you for your unconditional love you showed me and my family. I will keep on cooking the Christmas dinner each year with your Divine Guidance.

Jane in Virginia, thank you for your service to the world through your channeling every third Tuesday of the month and of course thank you for all you do.

My Dear Sai Maa. You are by far the most important person walking on this Earth whom I have the deepest respect and love for. Without your Divine presence and love in my life, I don't even know where I would be right now. I know The Profound Journey that you have created where you help get rid of peoples past pattern and get rid of the 'baggage' they carry, catapulted me into action. Today I am standing with a mission and a book finished and I owe it all to you. Om Jai Jai Sai Maa I will always love you.

Morfar (My grandfather) you are my hero and the person I always trusted for unconditional love and protection. I now know that you have been in my life to protect me and you have done that for several lifetimes. So it is no surprise that you are back in the family again. I love you and all you have ever done for me and can't wait to get our place back again. You know what I am talking about☺ Love you eternally.

I knew that the beautiful life that I had when I was with my Grandfather was somewhere and I thought it was 'out there'. When I found it coming out on the other side and seeing the light and love, I realized I have finally come 'home' to my 'self' and that I am love and light. I didn't need to go looking for it because 'it' was inside me all this time.

That feeling is within each one of us and that is where we find peace and love and 'home'.

So Dear Ones with love,

I am.

This is how much I love you all!!!!!

With Deep Gratitude.
Love Helene.

Made in the USA
San Bernardino, CA
23 February 2015